Confucius Says

— The Analects: Contents rearranged according to subject matter

Translated by lin Wusun

外文出版社
FOREIGN LANGUAGES PRESS

First Edition 2017

ISBNISBN 978-7-119-10543-7

Published by Foreign Languages Press Co. Ltd
24 Baiwanzhuang Road, Beijing 100037, China
http://www.flp.com.cn E-mail: flp@cipg.org.cn

Distributed by China International Book Trading Corporation
35 Chegongzhuang Xilu, Beijing 100044, China
P.O. Box 399, Beijing, China

Printed in the People's Republic of China

Preface to the Revised Edition of *Getting to Know Confucius —A New Translation of The Analects*

Several readers of my translation of *The Analects* have told me that while they remembered and related to many of the sayings of Confucius, they could not see the significance and relevance of many of his ideas to the world today.

I believe this is partly due to the fact that in *The Analects,* the core values of Confucius were not presented in a thematic way, but were scattered in different chapters. This is not Confucius' fault. *The Analects,* as is well-known, was put together by the Master's disciples and the disciples' disciples years after his death. The sayings and deeds of Confucius as well as some of his disciples were collated and most of them arranged without any theme, with a few passages even repetitive. I therefore hit upon the idea that perhaps I can help the readers by rearranging the passages in *The Analects* according to subject matter, with brief explanations for the major topics.

It is hoped that this will not only help the readers delve into the subject matter in a logical way, but also make it possible for readers to have a clearer idea of Confucius' thinking as well as the time he lived in.

However, this re-arrangement is easier said than done. Many of the passages touch on more than one topic and some could be put under different subject matters. Still others, though very few in number, could not be put under any subject matter. And the actual rearrangement requires a great amount of word processing work.

I was therefore very fortunate in that a young friend, Mr. Liu Bo, offered to help out on this tedious but exacting task. Without his dedication, I would not have been able to meet the time frame set by the publisher. I therefore owe Mr. Liu a great debt of gratitude.

In this edition, I have also revised the translation of some passages and added some footnotes to help readers better understand the original text. There is also a listing of the major events in Confucius' life and a map of his native and nearby states where Confucius and his disciples propagated his teachings.

In the world today, there is a growing interest in the Chinese language, culture and history. As many as 700 Confucius Institutes exist on the five con-tinents. And one hundred million people are studying the Chinese language. Along with this, interest in Confucius and his teachings is mounting year by year. In January this year, a new Sino-British-produced documentary on Confucius was shown on TV. In his book *On China*, Dr. Henry Kissinger took note of Confucius and his thinking as part of the background for an understanding of the Chinese psyche[1]. Without exaggeration, Confucius lives among us.

It is hoped that this revised English edition of *The Analects* will do its bit to make it easier for readers to grasp its significance and thus help promote international understanding and friendship among the nations and people of the world.

September, 2016

1 Chapter One, *The Singularity of China*, pp 5 & 32, *On China*, by Henry Kissinger, 2011.

Preface

The Analects, known as a classic on Confucius' teachings and experiences, was compiled by his disciples and second-generation disciples during the Spring and Autumn Period (722-480BC) in Chinese history. It is comprised of 20 separate "books", which are broken down into 492 passages. Though many of the passages are short, they often carry profound meaning.

For more than two thousand years, *The Analects* and Confucian thought have had an immeasurable impact on the Chinese people's thinking and Chinese culture. Confucian tradition constitutes the core and bedrock of the Chinese civilization, consistently making an impact on the development of China throughout history. Though Chinese students today no longer recite the *Four Books* and *Five Classics*, Confucian thought is still subtly influencing the ethos of the Chinese people. Confucianism is still very much alive with its positive values concerning society and ethics.

Centuries ago, missionaries who had been to China began to introduce *The Analects* to the West. With China's increasing influence abroad, *The Analects* and Confucius have evoked widespread interest in the world. Confucius and Confucianism belong not only to China but also to the entire world.

Mr. Lin, a celebrated translator in China, was the president of the China International Publishing Group some twenty years ago and is now an adviser to the Translators Association of China. He studied in India and in the United States and has actively engaged himself in promoting cross-cultural exchange throughout his career. Mr. Lin is therefore intimately aware of the different conceptual thoughts and reading habits of readers abroad and entertains his own ideas on bridging the gap between Chinese and Western cultures. Since the 1950s, he has worked in different fields of journalism and made remarkable achievements in translation. His translations, to mention a few, include *The Art of War by Sun Zi; The Art of War by Sun Bin*; *Riverside Talks: A Friendly Dialogue between A Christian and An Atheist*, and *Shanghai Pudong Miracle*. This book is yet another example of his applying cross-cultural understanding in solving translation difficulties.

Mr. Lin started the translation of *The Analects* in the late 1990s. Since then, he has read extensively Chinese and foreign books on *The Analects* as well as the latest studies in the field. Time and again, he revised his translation. To help foreign readers better understand *The Analects* and Confucian thought, he included in the book accounts about the life of Confucius, the development of Confucian thought, and the lasting influence of Confucius on Chinese philosophy and society. Mr. Lin also added necessary background information and explanatory notes to important passages and terminologies found in *The Analects*. In addition, to further help Western readers, Mr. Lin draws comparisons between Confucius, Socrates, and even Jesus, in their thoughts, experiences and influences.

A unique feature of this book is Mr. Lin's compilations of 30 useful quotations into a small pamphlet to be inserted in the book or carried separately for further study. This special design shows the translator's consideration for the readers and makes it so unusual among books on the same topic.

This new translation of *The Analects* by Mr. Lin Wusun will satisfy the needs of foreign readers in understanding Confucian thought and Chinese culture. It is hoped that every notable quotation from the book will resonate with the reader and help him appreciate the intricacies and practicality of Chinese philosophy.

"Rome was not built in one day," nor was this book. Upon the publication of this new translation of *The Analects*, I have the honor to write this preface to share with readers from around the world the cream of Chinese philosophy.

Zhou Mingwei
President
China International Publishing Group

Translator's Preface

In the late 1990s, I did my translation of *The Analects* in the beautiful seaside city of Qinhuangdao. However, since the Foreign Languages Press which commissioned me for the task changed its plan, I had time to add to my understanding of the original text by reading up on all the relevant academic works available to me. This process of deepening and regurgitation continued for over a decade during which I edited my own translation many times.

A word of explanation is needed as to why I describe my book as *a new translation*. It is new because it benefits from the latest research materials on *The Analects* published by Chinese academia.

I want specially to thank my wife Zhang Qingnian for her unflinching support and encouragement. She is the translation's first reader and her criticisms and suggestions did much to improve its faithfulness and readability.

Lin Wusun

November, 2009

CONTENT

Introduction

Who was Confucius?

Confucius[1] (551-491 BC) ranks the foremost among China's ancient thinkers. His teachings had a profound influence on the development of Chinese history and left a deep imprint on the Chinese psyche. He is also said to have initiated private tutoring, which constituted a forward step in Chinese education. Prior to him, there existed only official schools, the sole preserves for children of the aristocracy. People nowadays who are used to public education might not appreciate the full impact of private tutoring in those days as a revolutionary measure which helped to promote social mobility in ancient China. The introduction of the system of imperial examination whose content, during most periods in Chinese history, centered on Confucius' teachings, gave the children of different social background, particularly the under-privileged, a chance to pass the examination and move up the social ladder. To commemorate the Master, Confucius temples were built all over China, even down to the counties, the country's basic administrative unit.

Confucius lived during what is known as the Spring and Autumn

1 Latinized version of Kong Fuzi (Master Kong). His full name is Kong Qiu (孔丘).

Period (722-480 BC) in Chinese history. His native state was Lu, located in what is now Shandong Province in east China. At that time, the Zhou Dynasty (1030-211 BC) was in serious decline. Its rule was confined to a limited domain. The heads of its vassal states, whose rulers were mostly descendents of the king's close relatives and ministers, simply went their own way. These vassal states were constantly fighting among themselves, sometimes to the extent of the stronger conquering the weaker ones. Within these states, ministers often turned their rulers into puppets. Usurpations and palace coups were commonplace. It was in these tumultuous times that Confucius grew up. He therefore turned to the past to seek inspiration and role-models and to find cures for and solutions to current social ills. Many of the ancient concepts were developed and heroes reconstructed to fit in with Confucius' own philosophical and ethical ideas. And he called on the young to surpass the old. In this sense, he may be considered a traditionalist but not a conservative.

Confucius had a unique childhood. His father Shuliang Ge[1] was a warrior of rather low status. Generations back, one of his forefathers, a distinguished aristocrat by the name of Kong Fujia, had moved to the state of Lu from the neighboring state of Song to escape persecution after a palace coup there. Confucius' mother Yan Huizai was his father's third wife. Already in his 60s, Shuliang Ge had married her, a young woman from the capital, Qufu, in the hope that she would bear him a healthy son. She accomplished that, only to see her husband die when

1 Kong is his surname while Shuliang is his style name and Ge is his assumed name.

Confucius was only three. She then moved back home with her son and, despite a difficult life, devoted her entire energy to bringing up the child with distinction. Confucius did not fail his mother's expectations. His low social status did not prevent him from mastering the language skills, history and other branches of knowledge. A self-taught man, he took up various lowly jobs and avidly studied all the historical documents he could lay hands on. He thus became a widely-recognized scholar.

In this capacity, he began to teach while looking for official posts by offering advice to the rulers and high officials of Lu. Despite several failures, he did once become a senior official himself. However, when he tried to introduce reforms in accordance with his political doctrines, he met with strong resistance as these moves affected the vested interests of the officialdom. According to tradition, Confucius was appointed the Minister of Justice, but the duke of Lu and his chief minister stopped attending court when the neighboring state of Qi presented them with a troupe of singsong girls to distract them from Confucius' reform programs. He therefore decided to seek his political future abroad. He traveled to many states with his disciples and offered his service to their rulers. He was received with honor in several of the states. However, none took his advice seriously. Totally disappointed, he returned to Lu 14 years afterwards and spent the rest of his life teaching and editing ancient classics. His health impaired by the untimely death of his son and two of his most beloved disciples, he died at the age of 73, still convinced that he had a historic mission.

The Analects and Confucius' Ideas

The Analects — probably compiled after Confucius' death by his disciples and disciples' disciples who put their heads together to recollect what the Master had said and done — was originally in the form of wooden or bamboo strips. These were destroyed by order of Qin Shi Huang, the first emperor of Qin Dynasty (221-206 BC), who was a believer in legalism and authoritarian rule. Confucian scholars and texts perished in large numbers in his notorious campaign of extermination. Not long after, however, during the early Han Dynasty (206BC-220AD), Emperor Wudi adopted the Confucian doctrines at the advice of his minister, the scholar Dong Zhongshu, a move which contributed to the stability of his rule. From then on, Confucian ideas won the favor of the ruling class and therefore enjoyed a privileged position in China. As time went by, Confucius became idolized as a sage. Confucian temples were established in nearly every county. The most grandiose ones now still stand in the capital Beijing and in Confucius' native city, Qufu.

However, owing to Qin Shi Huang's persecution, only three versions of *The Analects* survived. One edition was in the State of Lu, and another in the neighboring Qi. Soon, one was discovered, hidden in the wall of the house of Confucius' descendents. *The Analects* we have today is an edited version which has probably experienced many changes through the ages. This can be proved as new versions of the classic have been found in ancient tombs by archeologists in recent years.

Confucius' overriding concern was the formation of a good government. To make this possible, he envisaged a virtuous and wise ruler who cared for his people and whose own meritorious behavior would make him a role-model for his ministers and subjects. He would surround himself with virtuous ministers and distance himself from unscrupulous servitors. At the bottom level, Confucius devised the formation of a harmonious family which he considered the nucleus of the society. There was a whole set of rules guiding the hierarchical relationship between father and son, between husband and wife, between elder and younger brothers and between friends. Trust, mutual concern and a sense of right and wrong were considered much more important and effective in weaving the social fabric than the implementation of strict rules and regulations. Life-long learning and continuous strivings to improve one's ethical standard would make one a man of honor worthy of admiration and emulation. That, he believed, would contribute to the making of an ideal society. A passage in *The Great Learning*, another Confucian classic taken from the ancient document *Li Ji* and edited by the Song Dynasty Confucian scholar, Zhu Xi (*1130-1200*), best epitomizes the above Confucian ethical-political ideal when it stated: Cultivate yourself and then your family will be put in order. When all the families achieve that, then the local government will be well run, and that will lead to peace and order in the whole country.

To us moderns, Confucius was not free of mistaken and out-dated ideas. His belittlement of women is notorious. Some current scholars tried to explain away his saying in this regard by giving us a different interpretation. However, this is not really necessary when we remember that Confucius lived in a patriarchal society where women had no social status and Confucius' attitude was merely a reflection of his time. Another passage showed him considering the common people too ignorant so that there was no need for one to bother with informing them of what was going on. Still another such anachronism was his low opinion of physical labor such as farming and even gardening. When his disciple Fan Chi asked him about his view on these matters, he answered he knew nothing about them, adding later that Fan Chi was indeed a petty man. The true question is how we should look at positive historical figures. However great they might be, they should not be put on a pedestal, prettified or glorified beyond their true selves. Confucius was what he was, a great thinker despite all his faults.

In *The Analects*, we find Confucius a very human figure, with his likes and dislikes, his hopes and disappointments, sometimes even a bit self-contradictory in his sayings. Confucius was convinced he had a great historic mission, given him by heavenly mandate. Yet he was so often disappointed that he sometimes lamented he was little understood. Once, he exclaimed that he was going to go overseas on a raft. On another occasion, he said it was not a bad idea to live among the tribal people.

After Confucius' death, his disciples dispersed to different states to spread his ideas, establishing various schools of thought themselves. Both Mencius and Xunzi were distinguished masters during the following Warring States period (475-221 BC). As time went by, there were different interpretations of Confucian ideas and this process has lasted ever since.

Confucius, Socrates and Jesus

For Western readers to fully appreciate Confucius, it is perhaps useful to touch on the commonalities as well as the differences between him and two leading lights of Western thought, i.e., Socrates and Jesus.

1. All three lived at times of crisis.

2. Both Confucius (551-491BC) and Socrates (469-399BC) lived in times which some Western historians called the Axial Age, when humankind began to ask some ultimate questions about life and the universe, about knowledge, truth and justice. Jesus came later, but he dealt with God and afterlife, and about the coming of the heavenly kingdom. Confucius, on the other hand, was a this-worldly thinker. Though he did believe in Heaven, destiny and the like, he avoided such subjects as the gods and supernatural forces. When asked about death, he answered that since we did not know enough about life, why should we bother about death and what happens afterwards. He never touched on what the Western people call ultimate questions like where we come from and where we are heading, or about afterlife. This characteristic mindset of his had a deep influence on the Chinese people.

3. All three were not appreciated while they lived and all three faced severe tests. Socrates was charged with the corruption of the Athenian youth and sentenced by the city court. He chose to drink hemlock instead

of being exiled. Jesus was crucified. Confucius died a natural death though he was never really given a chance to fulfill his self-determined mission.

4. All three became influential, thanks to the "missionary work" of their disciples and their ideas have since influenced the course of history. Confucius' ethical and political ideas, Socrates' analytical method aimed at probing the issues by dialogue and Jesus' compassion and his monotheism all became the most precious of the world's spiritual and cultural heritage.

5. In some ways, *The Analects* to the Chinese people before the end of the imperial dynasties in 1911 is as the Bible is to the Western people. One, it has left a deep imprint on the Chinese mindset, just as the Bible has on its readers in the West. Two, some similar ideas are expressed. For example, in the New Testament (Matthew) it says "Do unto others what you want them to do unto you". In *The Analects*, there is "Don't do unto others what you would not want others to do unto you", now known as the Golden Rule. Three, just as the Bible influenced the Western languages, *The Analects* enriched the Chinese language with many of its sayings and anecdotes, many of which are still very popular in daily use and in literary works. Four, tens of thousands of interpretations and annotations by scholars through the ages have been written about both works.

What was there in Confucius and his doctrines that made them so important?

To Confucius, politics and ethics formed an integral whole. He emphasized that one had first to learn how to improve himself and his relationship with others before he could run the government well. He therefore considered self-improvement a life-long process. To him, learning is not only limited to acquiring knowledge. It is mainly for upgrading one's own moral fiber and becoming a true man of honor.

However, it would be a mistake to consider Confucian ideas the sole trend of thought in traditional China. After Confucius' time and during the Warring States Period, there were many different schools of thought, such as those advocated by Laozi (Daoism, also translated as Taoism), Mozi (Moism) and Han Feizi (Legalism). In fact, there have been so many of them that it was described as a period where "a hundred schools of thought contend." At least a dozen of them were prominent. Later, Confucianism, Buddhism and Daoism (Taoism) came to the fore and they gradually achieved coexistence. However, throughout Chinese history, there were criticisms of Confucianism and some of these challenges represented brilliant gems in the history of ideas. And this was especially true during periods of turbulence.

The influence of Confucianism was not limited to China. For thousands of years, throughout East Asia, especially in Korea, Japan and vietnam, it enjoyed widespread recognition and today its impact on the local culture and politics can still be felt. This is especially noticeable in the island state of Singapore.

In modern China, when the country suffered severe defeats and setbacks at the hands of Western invaders, Chinese people, first of all the intellectuals, gradually came to the conclusion that something was seriously wrong with the country's basic political system, culture and ideology. That was the background to the May 4th New Cultural Movement of 1919 when democracy and science were introduced to the country and the slogan "Down with the Confucian Shop" was raised. It was a battle between the progressives, who wanted to introduce to China advanced Western ideas and systems to move the country ahead, and the conservatives, who wanted to keep China as it was. Confucianism was used by the latter as a rod to beat down the new radicals.

During modern Chinese history, there existed two camps on Confucius — pros and cons. Lu Xun, the influential modern progressive writer, and noted stateswoman Soong Ching Ling were both very critical of Confucius. Mao Zedong, on the other hand, once wrote that "We should sum up our history from Confucius to Sun Yat-sen and take over this valuable legacy."

The second time Confucius suffered a concerted attack was during the "Cultural Revolution" (1966-1976), but since the criticisms were so far-fetched and the true target of the campaign was some current political figures, it soon became a farce.

While Confucius was left alone in the years following the "Cultural Revolution", he soon became a subject of theoretical interest among scholars. The first serious attempt to restore Confucius' place in history was made in the 1980s by Kuang Yaming, a scholar and then president of Nanjing University. This was soon followed by the establishment of the Confucius Research Institute. Today, more and more, objective study has come to the fore.

However, what has really raised scholars' eyebrows is the fact that there has now appeared a mounting, popular fervor for Confucius and *The Analects.* Not only have lectures on Confucius become a great draw among university students, books on the subject have been published in hundreds of thousands of copies. A woman professor by the name of Yu Dan gave a series of TV lectures on Confucius and *The Analects.* This was followed by the publication of her book on the same topic. Both achieved phenomenal success. She was invited to speak in numerous cities, including Taipei, Seoul and Tokyo, and even in England. Meanwhile, other scholarly and popular books about Confucius and his teachings continue to hold the public's attention. A full-length feature film on Confucius directed by the famous woman director Hu Mei has been released and presented to the public with great fanfare. All signs show that the fervor for Confucius will rise still further. And it is interesting to note that China has established over 300 Confucius Institutes in 87 countries around the world within a few years, both to teach the Chinese language and Chinese culture. Internationally, too, there have been many new translations of *The Analects* and the study of Confucianism has made notable advances.

How can we explain Confucius' renewed popularity in China? It can be found in an analysis of several factors.

Firstly, if anything, the "Cultural Revolution" proved by negative example that tradition cannot be destroyed, whether by diktat or by mass movement, and that cultural values have a great staying power. In other words, it proved that the present, culturally as well as ideologically, can only be developed on the basis of the past, by sublimation rather than any other simplistic method. Secondly, now, 30 years after China's reform and opening up, the material well-being of most of its people has more or less been satisfied. What they need is some kind of political, spiritual and intellectual satisfaction. They need to find their cultural identity. In other words, the more prosperous the country becomes, the more people look for political, social, and cultural satisfactions. And for this, they need a new culture in line with the best of China's traditions. Simultaneously, the more prosperous and powerful China becomes, the greater its people's interest in the country's past. Along with the flood of post-modern pop cultures which has inundated the Chinese market, there is also a return to the country's cultural traditions. This has been amply demonstrated by renewed academic and popular interest in the past, the restoration of traditional holidays, and renewal of a good number of Chinese intangible cultural heritages including those of many ethnic groups. Studies of and attention to the Great Wall, the Terracotta soldiers, the Dunhuang Caves, the seven voyages (1405-1433AD) of Admiral Zheng He during the Ming Dynasty[1], for example, have also

1 His voyages to Southeast Asia, India and Africa predate Columbus' voyages (1492-1498) by more than 50 years.

increased.

Let us cite an example of how the best of Confucian ideas is being developed to form one of China's basic state policies. The call for a harmonious society at home and a harmonious world can be traced back to Confucius' principles of "harmony is precious" (和为贵), "harmony but not sameness" (和而不同) and "a myriad things, each following its own course without interfering with others" (道并行而不相悖). This policy has won widespread recognition because experience has proved that it serves the basic interests of people the world over.

Several questions need clarification before we proceed further.

One, Confucianism need not be mutually exclusive with regard to other philosophical theories and religions. It has existed alongside Buddhism and Daoism for millennia. In fact, they even interpenetrated each other.

Today, many Chinese thinkers have absorbed the best of those teachings for their own benefit and for the service of the people.

Two, Confucianism, as an ethical theory, is unique, but when we study it closely, we find that it has many points in common with Christianity and other religions. Examples are legion. For instance, you will find the different religions all have their own sayings about the Golden Rule, i.e., "Don't do unto others what you would not like others do unto you." So we can say that the different civilizations need not be mutually exclusive. They can and need to coexist in our present inter-connected world, for so close are the different nations to each other that the world has truly become a global village.

Three, in our age, while congratulating ourselves on our phenomenal advances, we are at the same time humbled by the reverses our humankind has experienced. More than ever we are painfully aware of the fact that our knowledge of the world, the universe and the cosmos is still very limited and that we still have a long way to go in our quest for truth. In both natural and social sciences, there are still many unexplored fields. In economics, as the recent financial crisis has shown, we are still groping in the dark in some areas and on some matters, and no economy has proved to be faultless. It would be more intellectually honest and beneficial to be open-minded and to try and draw from the best of the different theories and sublimate them.

Four, in China today, what we are witnessing throughout the 30 years of opening-up and reform is just such a process — absorbing the best from different theories and applying them according to Chinese conditions. The development of socialism and the advance in material wealth is accompanied by the stress on morality, the growth of religious beliefs and the throwback to tradition alongside the intake of Western ideas. Western and traditional Chinese medicine (TCM), Western classical music and ballet alongside Chinese traditional music, Peking Opera and a variety of local operas, Chinese cuisine of all sorts and international cuisines all have their place in China, to cite only a few examples. Life, as in the case of Nature, becomes multifarious and colorful. So, too, the world's development approaches and social systems. There is no single universal model. While there do exist universal values, their application depends very much on the uniqueness of each local condition, the differing social and historical situation in different parts of the world. The great commonality which Confucius spoke of and which was expounded by the scholar/reformer Kang Youwei of the late Qing Dynasty and the early Republic as well as by Dr. Sun Yat-sen, the founding father of the Chinese Republic, is a vision which nobody knows when it would materialize.

What can readers from abroad who are interested in China learn from *The Analects*? Young readers may enrich their knowledge and vision by reading this ancient classic. They will find Confucius a friend who crossed the time channel to provide them with much worldly wisdom. Those interested in Chinese culture and plan to work in China will find in it useful tips to Chinese people's values, such as the stress on family and on human relationship, respect for the elderly and the great attachment to learning and moral self-improvement. This latter is significant since the majority of the Chinese people are not religious believers, yet there is amongst them a strong sense of right and wrong inherited from their early family influence and school education where, if we look close enough, we can still find some pervading influence of Confucian thought.

To conclude, we might offer a bit of advice: Don't read *The Analects* for the sake of reading. The current world, both in China and in other parts of the globe, is so different from the times of Confucius. There are components of his teaching which are outdated. But some of his ideas still carry great weight when we look into their deeper meanings. In other words, make use of *The Analects* as is applicable to your own situation.

And you will benefit greatly from your encounter with Confucius.

Confucius' Disciples

Since a good number of the passages in *The Analects* are in the form of dialogue between Confucius and his disciples, it is important to familiarize our readers with the names and character of some of the disciples.

Tradition has it that during his lifetime, Confucius had 3,000 disciples, of whom 72 were the most prominent. That may be an exaggeration as the Master took students regardless of their social status. He did not run a school as we understand the term today. He either led them in discussions or answered their questions individually. Some scholars claim that "his disciples" included his disciples' disciples. If that was so, then the figure 3,000 might be justified. Whatever the case, among the 72 disciples, only 29 were mentioned in *The Analects.*

Before we list them, we need to explain how Chinese names, especially those ancient names, are formed.

1. Chinese names are confusing to English-language speakers for more than one reason. First of all, the Chinese surname comes before the given name.
2. Up till modern times, literate Chinese often had more than one name. Besides his surname and given name, he had a style name (字*zi*), which his friends often used when talking

or referring to him, and several assumed names (号 *hao*). For example, Zilu (子路), one of Confucius' leading disciples, is known in *The Analects* as *1*) Zhong You (仲由), which is his real name, *2*) You (由), *3*) Zilu (子路) and *4*) Jilu (季路) ("Ji" denoting that he was the fourth son in the family). To simplify matters, we have stuck to one name for each person in the translation.

In the following listing, we will give a brief description of a few of Confucius' disciples. This will help show the different relationship the Master had with his disciples, and also give some insight on why Confucius sometimes expressed different ideas on the same subject. The Master picked his words and explanations according to the level of understanding of his disciples. For example, he gave different answers to different disciples when they asked the same question of what the term "humaneness" meant.

1. Yan Hui (颜回) was the Master's most favorite disciple. Extremely poor but very studious, he followed Confucius' lessons carefully and with whom he never had any disagreement. His early death certainly affected his influence in the spread of the Master's teaching.
2. Zilu (子路) was in many ways the opposite of Yan Hui. He was eager to express his views in front of the Master, He was outspoken, straight-forward, not afraid to express different views and even criticized Confucius despite his loyalty to the sage.

He was courageous even to the point of rashness. Zilu died in battle while still middle-aged. He was a heroic figure, but he, too, had little influence in propagating Confucius' ideas.

3. Zigong (子贡) was perhaps the most eloquent of the Master's disciples. Unlike Yan Hui, he came from a prosperous family. He took up office several times and distinguished himself by his business acumen.

4. Zeng Cen (曾参) was known as Master Zeng to Confucius' second-generation disciples. He stressed the importance of filial piety and had great influence in the spread of Confucian thought.

5. Zixia (子夏), like Zeng Cen, was one of Confucius' younger disciples. He was eloquent and was noted for his literary achievements. After the Master's death, he, along with Zigong and Zeng Cen, played a leading role in spreading Confucius' teachings.

6. Ranyou (冉由) looked very much like Confucius and once even pretended to be his Master, only to be exposed when he could not answer his fellow disciples' questions. After Confucius' death, Ran You was among those disciples who tried to make Confucius a sage, although the Master never claimed to be one. In *The Analects*, he sometimes appeared as Master You.

Yan Hui, Zeng Cen and Ranyou were the Master's favorites because they were quick in understanding his ideas and their implications, few in words, careful in action. In short, different yet future models of a man of honor.

Terminology in *The Analects*

In *The Analects*, Confucius employed a good number of terms to express his ideas on what was good ethics and good politics. Many of these terms appeared in earlier classics, like *The Book of Songs, Yi Ching and Spring and Autumn*, but Confucius endowed them with new meanings. However, since Confucius only described but never defined them and since he gave different answers to the same terms depending on his disciples' individual characters and level of understanding, it is very difficult to determine their exact definitions. Besides, as Classical Chinese is very concise and lends to different interpretations, there is no single English equivalent to these terms. For example, *ren* (仁) has been translated as benevolence, humanity, goodness, etc., *li* (礼) as ritual propriety rites and rituals, *junzi* (君子) as gentleman and, exemplary person and *xiaoren* (小人) as petty man, common man and vulgar man. All this lends to different interpretation and causes confusion. Below, I give my own renditions as well as the reasons for my choice. I hope they will help readers gain insight into Confucius' basic concepts and, therefore, his teachings.

1. *Junzi* (君子) literally means "son of the ruler", and therefore refers to a member of the aristocracy. In *The Analects*, the term

was used by Confucius to describe his ideal person, the type who through self-improvement, becomes superior in ethics, gains peace of mind and therefore is fit to govern. To Confucius, people of low social ranks but willing to study and improve themselves can become *junzi,* whereas those scholars who are morally unfit cannot, thus giving the term strong ethical implications. *Junzi* has been translated as gentleman, but he is not the gentleman as used in today's English. In the present translation, I am using a "person of honor" to emphasize the difference and denote its ethical character.

2. *Xiaoren* (小人) literally means the people of low social status, or common people, but Confucius used it mostly to refer to those who had petty interest in mind. In this translation, I am using "petty-minded people", and only occasionally "petty people" Here again, "petty-mindedness" has an ethical implication.
3. *Shi* (士) refers to the lowest echelon of the aristocracy. With their knowledge, they could become officials if they enjoyed the appreciation of the rulers. But then, the majority would retain their original status. Here, to simplify matters, I am following the traditional English rendition "scholar".
4. *Ren* (仁) is rendered in this translation as humaneness. The simplest explanation Confucius gave to his disciple for this term was "To love others." The most famous quotation is "Don't do unto others what you do not want others to do unto you." Elsewhere, he stressed that what one wanted to achieve he

should help others achieve too. However, Confucius did not advocate universal love. This can be understood as he lived in a stratified society with different status.

5. *Li* (礼) is rather broad in content. It includes rituals, etiquette, regulations and rules of proper behavior. During Confucius' time, there was no official law as we understand it today, but people would be punished when they violated the rules and regulations. Confucius paid great attention to *Li* which was set down when the Zhou Dynasty was first established. He believed that the neglect of *Li* was the cause of all troubles of that time. The ministers neglected it at random and without any sense of shame, and their stewards and the society at large were followed their examples. Confucius therefore considered it his mission to advise those in power to correct their ways through following *Ren* and restoring *Li*. The two concepts are closely related, the former being the kernel while the latter its outer form.
6. *Yue* (乐) is simply translated as music. In Confucius' time, there was a strict rule as to what kind of music was to be played in court and, performed before visiting state leaders and on ceremonious occasions. It was therefore very important to handle it properly as it was considered to be a great booster of *Li*. Poems in *The Book of Songs*, China's most ancient collection of poetry, were often sung and accompanied by music. Confucius was a great lover of music and often discussed with his disciples

its intricacy and significance. Confucius considered it his task to teach the people *Li* and *Yue* which he believed would help people to achieve *Ren* and promote stability in society.

7. *Xiao* (孝) is filial piety. In the patriarchal society, the father had absolute power in the family, and the children's love and respect for him was considered very important. Related to this was the respect for the brothers, especially the eldest one, because he would take over the family after the father's death. This is called *Ti* (悌). Since the family, the basic unit of society, carried great weight during Confucius' time, he made *Xiao* and *Ti* basic ethical traits underpinning the society's stability, stressing that with them, no filial son would cause trouble and start a revolt against the state.
8. *De* (德) is virtue, still one of the most popular terms in present-day China. Recently, the Chinese government has raised the slogan of building a virtuous government (德政) to better run the country.
9. *Dao* (道) is usually rendered in English as "the Way". Its literal meaning is path or road, implying that one needs to master the true way of life and nature. It was widely used by ancient Chinese thinkers, whose most well-known works to the West were *Daodejing* (《道德经》), also known as *Laozi* and *The Art of War* by Sunzi.
10. *Yi* (义) has many different English translations. The Chinese meaning is justice and righteousness, representing a kind of

internal restraint. We have used "justice" "appropriateness" and "righteousness", depending on the context.

11. *Xin* (信) is rendered here as "trust", meaning "keep one's word in human relationship". "Trustworthy" is also used when the occasion requires.
12. *Tian* (天) implies the master of Nature and humankind. And the emperors called themselves "sons of heaven" (天子). *Tian* does not have the meaning as in some religions where God lives and where good people go when they die. To simplify matters, we use heaven while reminding readers of the difference. In *The Analects,* the mandate of heaven (天命) is often used.

In conclusion, live the present, look to the future, but build on the past, that is a sure way to enrich one's life and achieve harmony within and without. That is the lesson I learnt reading and translating Confucius. I would like to share it with you, our readers.

一

仁 *ren*

I

Humaneness

Confucius on Humaneness (仁 *ren*)

How can we lead a good life and improve ourselves? How should we treat each other? And how should a state be governed? These are issues that Confucius was especially concerned about. And humaneness is Confucius' key concept and core value when answering these questions. Among the 500-odd passages in *The Analects*, 56 are concerned with his answers to this concept and the word humaneness appears 109 times. Confucius gave no definition as to what he meant by humaneness. However, there were three occasions when, answering inquiries from his disciples, he did explain his understanding of humaneness. In one case, in the plainest answer of all, he said, "One who is humane loves other people." In another passage, he said, "He who helps others to establish what he himself wishes to establish and to achieve what he himself wishes to achieve is a humane person." In still another, he gave the now famous dictum that "Do not do unto others what you would not wish others do unto you."

To make himself clear, Confucius also noted that there were qualities

7.30 *

子曰:“仁远乎哉?我欲仁,斯仁至矣。”

12.2

仲弓问仁。子曰:“出门如见大宾,使民如承大祭。己所不欲,勿施于人;在邦无怨,在家无怨。”

仲弓曰:“雍虽不敏,请事斯语矣。”

---

* 为避免内容误读,本书每段内容均以原著章节标注。

and behaviors which are ethically recommendable but could not be considered as humaneness. He also gave concrete examples of people whom he considered humane.

Confucius emphasized that people were not born with humaneness and that it had to be cultivated with effort and persistence. To Confucius, children were reared in the family with love and concern and as they grew up, they responded with the same feeling for their parents and siblings and through self-cultivation that feeling of love was extended to other members of the society. In this respect, it should be noted that Confucius lived in a class society and, while he did express concern for the underclass, he did not call for complete social equality.

7.30* The Master said, "Is humaneness really so remote? I've only to wish for it and it will come to me."

12.2 Zhong Gong asked about humaneness. The Master said, "In public, act as if you were receiving an honored guest. While employing the services of the common people, act as if you were officiating a major ceremony. Do not do unto others what you would not wish others do unto you. In this way, you will incur no bitter feelings against you whether in state or family affairs.

Zhong Gong said, "Though I am not intelligent, I shall follow what you have just said."

---

* To avoid misunderstanding about the context, each passage is headed by a numeral noting the original chapter and passage.

§1.1 何以谓“仁”？

1.3

子曰：巧言令色，鲜仁矣。”（见 *17.17*）

3.3

子曰：“人而不仁，如礼何？人而不仁，如乐何？”

3.8

子夏问曰：“‘巧笑倩兮，美目盼兮，素以为绚兮’。何谓也？”

子曰：“绘事后素。”

曰：“礼后乎？”

子曰：“起予者商也，始可与言诗已矣。”

4.2

子曰：“不仁者不可以久处约，不可以长处乐。仁者安仁，知者利仁。”

4.5

子曰：“富与贵，是人之所欲也，不以其道得之，不处也；贫与贱，是人之所恶也，不以其道得之，不去也。君子去仁，恶乎成名？君子无终食之间违仁，造次必于是，颠沛必于是。”

§ 1.1 What constitutes humaneness and what does not?

1.3 The Master said, "A smooth tongue and an ingratiating manner are seldom signs of being humane." (The same passage appeared in *17.17*)

3.3 The Master said, "What have the rituals got to do with a person who is not humane? What have music and dance (乐 *yue*) got to do with him?"

3.8 Zixia asked about the connotation of a verse in the *Book of Songs*. "The pretty dimples of the artful smile, the well-defined black and white of the eyes, are like colorful patterns on plain silk."
The Master answered, "Only when you have a white base, can you paint colors on it."
Zixia said, "Can we then conclude that likewise, regulations and rituals come after humaneness?"
The Master said, "Zixia, you have thrown new light on this verse for me. I can now discuss the *Book of Songs* with you."

4.2 The Master said, "He who lacks humaneness can neither be content in poverty nor be happy for long in wealth. A man of honor rests at ease with humaneness, while a wise man chooses humaneness because it is advantageous for him to do so."

4.5 The Master said, "Wealth and rank are what men desire, but the man of honor would not accept them unless they are obtained in a proper way. Poverty and lowliness are what men detest, but the man of honor would not try to get rid of them by means of an improper method. How can one be called a man of honor if he forsakes humaneness? Never for a moment should he do that. The man of honor clings to humaneness whether in moments of haste

4.6

子曰:“我未见好仁者，恶不仁者。好仁者，无以尚之；恶不仁者，其为仁矣，不使不仁者加乎其身。有能一日用其力于仁矣乎？我未见力不足者。盖有之矣，我未之见也。”

4.7

子曰:“人之过也，各于其党。观过，斯知仁矣。”

5.12

子贡曰:“我不欲人之加诸我也，吾亦欲无加诸人。”

子曰:“赐也，非尔所及也。”

6.19

曰:“人之生也直，罔之生也幸而免。”

6.30

子贡曰:“如有博施于民而能济众，何如？可谓仁乎？”

子曰:“何事于仁？必也圣乎！尧舜其犹病诸。夫仁者，己欲立而立人，己欲达而达人。能近取譬，可谓仁之方也已。”

or in times of hardship."

4.6 The Master said, "I have yet to meet a man who truly loves humaneness, or a person who detests another because he lacks humaneness. He who detests those lacking in humaneness feels so because he does not want to be contaminated by what is inhumane. Is there anyone who can achieve humaneness through his efforts in a single day? I have never seen anyone who has that capacity. Perhaps there are, but I have yet to see one like that."

4.7 The Master said, "There are all types of people and all types of faults. Each one's faults can be traced to the type of people he belongs to. By analyzing his faults, you will come to know the type of person he is."

5.12 Zigong said, "I don't want to do to others what I don't want them to do to me."

The Master commented, "Zigong, you have yet to live up to that saying."

6.19 The Master said, "Man is born to be upright. He who is not upright survives by mere chance."

6.30 Zigong asked the Master, "What do you think of someone who gives extensively to the common people and provides aid to the multitude? Would you say he is humane?"

The Master answered, "He is far more than being humane. He must be a sage. Even Yao and Shun could not have done as much. A humane person is one who helps others establish what he himself wishes to establish and to achieve what he himself wishes to achieve. To be able to correlate one's own feelings with those of others may be the best way to approach humaneness."

8.10

子曰:“好勇疾贫，乱也。人而不仁，疾之已甚，乱也。”

8.11

子曰:“如有周公之才之美，使骄且吝，其余不足观也已。”

12.3

司马牛问仁。子曰:“仁者，其言也讱（rèn）。”

曰:“其言也讱，斯谓之仁已乎?”

子曰:“为之难，言之得无讱乎?”

12.15

子曰:“博学于文，约之以礼，亦可以弗畔矣夫!”(同 6.27)

13.19

樊迟问仁。子曰:“居处恭，执事敬，与人忠。虽之夷狄，不可弃也。”

13.27

子曰:“刚、毅、木、讷近仁。”

14.1

宪问耻。子曰:“邦有道，谷;邦无道，谷，耻也。”

“克、伐、怨、欲不行焉，可以为仁矣?”

8.10 The Master said, "Those who are brave but cannot tolerate poverty are likely to cause trouble. So are those who lack virtue and are despised."

8.11 The Master said, "Should a man as gifted as the Duke of Zhou be arrogant and niggardly, then his other qualities are not worth looking at."

12.3 Sima Niu[1] asked about humaneness. The Master said, "A humane person is cautious with his words."

Sima Niu asked, "Does that mean a man who is cautious with his words can be regarded as humane?"

The Master said, "How can a man not be cautious with his words when it is so difficult to turn his words into deeds?"

12.15 The Master said, "The humane will not go astray for he is widely read and he keeps himself in line with the rituals." (The same passage appeared in *6.27*)

13.19 Fan Chi asked about humaneness. The Master said, "Be courteous in daily life, conscientious at work and honest and sincere toward others. These are qualities which cannot be forsaken even if you go and live among the uncultivated tribes."

13.27 The Master said, "Being staunch, resolute, modest and deliberate in speech makes one almost a humane person."

14.1 Yuan Si asked about shame. The Master answered, "When the Way prevails in the state, it is alright to take office for pay. However, it would be shameful to take office when the Way does not prevail."

"Would someone be considered humane if he has overcome

1 Confucius' disciple.

子曰:“可以为难矣，仁则吾不知也。”

14.4

子曰:“有德者必有言，有言者不必有德。仁者必有勇，勇者不必有仁。”

§1.2　何以至“仁”？

4.1

子曰:“里仁为美。择不处仁，焉得知？”

12.21

樊迟从游于舞雩之下，曰:“敢问崇德、修慝（tè)、辨惑。”

子曰:“善哉问！先事后得，非崇德与？攻其恶，无攻人之恶，非修慝与？一朝之忿，忘其身以及其亲，非惑与？”

12.22

攀迟问仁。子曰:“爱人。”

问知。子曰:“知人。”樊迟未达。子曰:“举直错诸枉，能使枉者直。”

the faults of trying to be better than others, of bragging about himself, of bearing grudges against others and of being covetous?"

The Master answered, "It would be difficult to become such a person, but even then, I don't know if he can be considered humane."

14.4 The Master said, "A virtuous man is sure to be eloquent; but an eloquent man is not necessarily virtuous. A humane person is sure to be courageous; but a courageous man is not necessarily humane."

§ 1.2 How to achieve humaneness.

4.1 The Master said, "It is beautiful to have your mind set on achieving humaneness. How can one say you are wise if you fail to do that?"

12.21 Fan Chi accompanied Confucius on an outing to the Rain Altar. He said, "May I ask how one can cultivate virtue, clear up resentment against oneself and recognize foolishness?"

The Master answered, "What an excellent question! Isn't a person cultivating virtue when he places service before reward? Isn't he clearing up resentment when he criticizes his own mistakes rather than those of others? Isn't it foolishness when, in a sudden fit of anger, one neglects his own safety and even that of his parents?"

12.22 Fan Chi asked about humaneness. The Master said, "Love your fellow men."

He asked about wisdom. The Master said, "Know your fellow men." Seeing that Fan Chi failed to grasp his meaning, the

樊迟退，见子夏曰：“乡也吾见于夫子而问知，子曰‘举直错诸枉，能使枉者直’，何谓也？”

子夏曰：“富哉言乎！舜有天下，选于众，举皋陶（gāoyáo），不仁者远矣。汤有天下，选于众，举伊尹，不仁者远矣。”

15.10

子贡问为仁。子曰：“工欲善其事，必先利其器。居是邦也，事其大夫之贤者，友其士之仁者。”

17.6

子张问仁于孔子。孔子曰：“能行五者于天下为仁矣。”

“请问之。”曰：“恭、宽、信、敏、惠。恭则不侮，宽则得众，信则人任焉，敏则有功，惠则足以使人。”

§ 1.3 “仁”之形态

6.23

子曰：“知者乐（yào）水，仁者乐山；知者动，仁者静；知者乐，仁

Master added, "Promote the righteous and set them over the unrighteous. That can make the unrighteous righteous."
Fan Chi withdrew and went to see Zixia, saying, "Just now I asked the Master about wisdom and he said, 'Promote the righteous and set them over the unrighteous. That will make the unrighteous righteous.' What did he mean?"
Zixia said, "How rich the meaning of his words! When Shun took over the rein, he promoted Gao Yao from the ranks and by so doing, he kept those who were not humane at bay. When Tang took over the rein, he promoted Yi Yin from the ranks and, by so doing, kept those who were not humane at bay."

15.10 Zigong wanted to know how to practise humaneness. The Master said, "A craftsman must first sharpen his tools if he is to do his work well. Whichever state you happen to be in, serve the most virtuous of the ministers and befriend the most humane of the scholars."

17.6 Zizhang asked Confucius about humaneness. Confucius said, "Whoever applies the five qualities to all under Heaven is humane."
"What are these five qualities?"
"Courtesy, tolerance, good faith, agility and generosity. Courtesy frees you from insults, tolerance wins the hearts of many, good faith secures the trust of others, agility leads to success and generosity gives one authority to employ others."

§ 1.3 What are its main manifestations?

6.23 The Master said, "The wise love the waters, the humane love the mountains. The wise love activity, the humane tranquility. The

者寿。”

9.1

子罕言利，与命与仁。

9.29

子曰：“知者不惑，仁者不忧，勇者不惧。”

15.9

子曰：“志士仁人，无求生以害仁，有杀身以成仁。”

15.35

子曰：“民之于仁也，甚于水火。水火，吾见蹈而死者矣，未见蹈仁而死者也。”

15.36

子曰：“当仁，不让于师。”

§1.4　仁者之仁

4.3

子曰：“唯仁者能好（hào）人，能恶人。”

4.4

子曰：“苟志于仁矣，无恶也。”

4.22

子曰：“古者言之不出，耻躬之不逮也。”

wise enjoy life; the humane are blessed with longevity."

9.1 Seldom did the Master touch on the subjects of personal gain, but not so with regard to fate and humaneness.

9.29 The Master said, "The wise are not perplexed, the humane do not worry and the brave have no fear."

15.9 The Master said, "Those with public spirit and lofty ideals will not try to save their lives at the expense of humaneness. They will readily give up their lives for its sake."

15.35 The Master said, "Humaneness is more vital to the common people than fire and water. I have seen people die in fire and water, but I have never seen anyone die by following the course of humaneness."

15.36 The Master said, "Where humaneness is concerned, be not afraid to overtake your master."

§ 1.4 The humaneness of the humane person.

4.3 The Master said, "Only the humane knows how to love and how to hate."

4.4 The Master said, "He who sets his mind on achieving humaneness will be free from evil-doing."

4.22 The Master said, "The ancients were sparing in words, because they were afraid their deeds might not live up to their words."

二

礼：礼节、习俗、风俗及社会关系准则

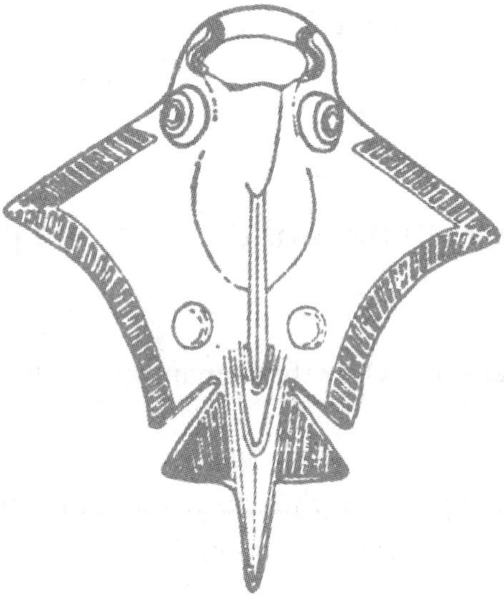

II

Ritual Propriety — Social Mores, Etiquette, Customs and Rules Governing Social Relationship

Confucius on Rituals and Ritual Propriety (礼 *Li*)

The character Li (礼) was originally used for sacrificial and social ceremonies. Confucius, however, extended its meaning to include both institutional and conceptual ones, thus embracing one's attitude towards one's superiors (parent, teachers, officials and rulers) as well as behavioral patterns accepted as appropriate in a community, including what we call today etiquette, customs, manners, etc.

To Confucius, there is a close tie between ritual propriety and humaneness. He stressed that if one was not humane, then there would be for him no ritual propriety to speak of. Confucius was a great admirer of the rules and regulations, customs and etiquette established during the early years of the Zhou Dynasty. He thought that with the restoration of the Zhou Li, the problems bedeviling his times would be solved. So he declared, "To restrain oneself and observe the rituals constitute humaneness. Once you have done that then every land under heaven

3.1

孔子谓季氏，“八佾舞于庭，是可忍也，孰不可忍也！”

3.2

三家者以《雍》彻。子曰：“‘相维辟公，天子穆穆’，奚取于三家之堂？”

3.6

季氏旅于泰山，子谓冉有曰：“女弗能救与？”

对曰：“不能。”子曰：“呜呼！曾谓泰山不如林放乎？”

3.10

子曰：“禘（dì）自既灌而往者，吾不欲观之矣。”

3.21

哀公问社于宰我，宰我对曰：“夏后氏以松，殷人以柏，周人以栗，曰：使民战栗。”

will be ruled by humaneness."

3.1 The Master spoke thus of Jisun[1]. "He had eight rows of dancers perform for him in his courtyards. If this violation of the rituals can be tolerated, what cannot be?"

3.2 The three noble families of Lu had the *Yong* song[2] performed while their sacrificial offerings were being removed. The Master said, "It is said in the *Book of Songs* that 'With dukes in attendance, the Son of Heaven showed great solemnity when offering sacrifices.' How then is this song appropriate?"

3.6 Jisun intended to offer sacrifices to Heaven on Mount Tai. On learning about this, the Master asked Ranyou[3], "Can't you stop him from doing that?" When Ranyou answered he couldn't, the Master said, "Alas, can it be that the God of Mount Tai knows less about the rituals than Lin Fang?"[4]

3.10 The Master said, "After the first offering of wine, I don't want to go on watching the Di ceremony."[5]

3.21 Duke Ai of Lu asked Zaiwo[6] what kind of timber to use when making a memorial tablet for the God of Earth. Zaiwo answered, "Xia used pinewood, Yin used cedar and Zhou used chestnut. It

1 One of the three families, namely Mengsun, Shusun and Jisun, who were then the most powerful nobles in the State of Lu.

2 A song reserved for royal occasions.

3 Confucius' disciple.

4 Lin Fang knew the rituals of the Zhou Dynasty, according to which only the king had the right to make offers to Heaven on Mount Tai. Since Jisun was only a noble, he had no right to do so. Therefore, the God of Mount Tai would not accept Jisun's sacrifice.

5 A ceremony for offering sacrifices to ancestors. Conducting the Di ceremonial service was reserved as the sole right of the King. Hence Confucius could not bear to see it conducted by the duke of the State of Lu.

6 Confucius' disciple.

子闻之，曰："成事不说，遂事不谏，既往不咎。"

3.26

子曰："居上不宽，为礼不敬，临丧不哀，吾何以观之哉？"

15.1

卫灵公问陈于孔子。孔子对曰："俎（zǔ）豆之事，则尝闻之矣；军旅之事，未之学也。"明日遂行。

16.14

邦君之妻，君称之曰夫人，夫人自称曰小童；邦人称之曰君夫人，称诸异邦曰寡小君；异邦人称之亦曰君夫人。

17.11

子曰："礼云礼云，玉帛云乎哉？乐云乐云，钟鼓云乎哉？"

17.18

子曰："恶紫之夺朱也，恶郑声之乱雅乐也，恶利口之覆邦家者。"

is said that using the wood of the chestnut tree will cause the common people to tremble in awe.[1]

Hearing this, the Master commented, "One should not explain what has been done, nor should he try to advise against what is already accomplished. What's done is done."

3.26 The Master said, "I cannot put up with a person who, while in high position, is lacking in tolerance, and who shows no reverence while performing the rituals and feels no grief while in mourning."

15.1 When Duke Ling of Wei asked Confucius about military tactics, Confucius replied, "I have some knowledge about the regulations and rituals. As to military affairs, I have never studied them." He left Wei the next day.

16.14 The ruler of a state calls his wife "my lady." When she talks to her husband, she calls herself "your little one." The people of the state refer to her as "the lord's lady." When going abroad, the ruler calls her "my little lord." People of other states use the term "the lord's lady" when referring to her.

17.11 The Master said, "They talk of the rituals, but surely these are not limited to the ceremonial presentation of jade and silk. They talk of music, but surely it is not limited to the playing of bells and drums."

17.18 The Master said, "I detest purple replacing vermillion. I detest the pop tunes of Zheng replacing classical music. I detest the

1 Here Zaiwo is using a pun, because the "chestnut tree" and "tremble in awe" are homonyms in Chinese.

§ 2.1 “礼”“仁”之道

1.9

曾子曰:“慎终追远，民德归厚矣。”

4.23

子曰:“以约失之者鲜矣。”

12.1

颜渊问仁。子曰:“克己复礼为仁。一日克己复礼，天下归仁焉。为仁由己，而由人乎哉?”

颜渊曰:“请问其目。”子曰:“非礼勿视，非礼勿听，非礼勿言，非礼勿动。”颜渊曰:“回虽不敏，请事斯语矣。”

clever tongues subverting states and noble families."[1]

§ 2.1 Relationship between humaneness and ritual propriety.

1.9 Master Zeng said, "When funerals for parents are conducted strictly in accordance with the rituals and sacrifices to ancestors offered devoutly, then the morals of the common people will naturally thrive."

4.23 The Master said, "Seldom does a man of restraint make mistakes."

12.1 Yan Hui asked about humaneness. The Master said, "To restrain oneself and observe the rituals constitute humaneness. Once you have done these, the world will consider you humane. However, the practice of humaneness depends on no one but yourself." Yan Hui then asked, "What are the essentials of humaneness?" The Master answered, "Do not look unless it is in accordance with the rituals, do not listen unless it is in accordance with the rituals, do not speak unless it is in accordance with the rituals, do not do anything that is not in accordance with the rituals." Yan Hui said, "Though I am not intelligent, I shall stick to what you have just said."

1 In ancient times, vermillion was considered the pure color. During the Spring and Autumn Period, some lords turned to dressing in purple. As a result, purple replaced vermillion as the pure color. Hence Confucius' reproach.

§ 2.2 “礼”之精髓

1.13

有子曰：“信近于义，言可复也；恭近于礼，远耻辱也；因不失其亲，亦可宗也。”

5.18

子曰：“臧文仲居蔡，山节藻棁（zhuō），何如其知也！

3.3

子曰：“人而不仁，如礼何？人而不仁，如乐何？”

3.4

林放问礼之本。子曰：“大哉问！礼，与其奢也，宁俭；丧，与其易也，宁戚。”

3.7

子曰：“君子无所争，必也射乎！揖让而升，下而饮，其争也君子。”

§ 2.2 The essence of ritual propriety.

1.13 Master You said, "So long as a promise is in line with righteousness (义 *yi*), it should be kept. So long as respect conforms with rituals, it will keep humiliation at a distance. It follows that relying on those with whom one has close relationship[1] is dependable."

5.18 The Master said, "Zang Wenzhong[2] kept a large tortoise in his house and for this pet, he had hills painted on the pillars and duckweeds on the raft posts. What is one to think of his intelligence?"[3]

3.3 The Master said, "What have the rituals got to do with a person who is not humane? What have music and dance (乐 *yue*) got to do with him?"

3.4 Lin Fang[4] asked about the essence of the rituals. The Master answered, "What a good question that is! When performing a ritual, it is better to be frugal than to be extravagant. In mourning, it is more important to be really grief-stricken than to go through all the solemn formalities."

3.7 The Master said, "There is no contention between two men of honor. The only exception is perhaps archery. Even so, when the contest starts, the two archers bow to make way for each other.

---

1 It is not clear whether Master You was referring to one's kins or to people with similar views.

2 A minister of Lu.

3 The ancients in China worshipped the tortoise for its longevity, the bigger they were, the more precious. Here, Confucius was critical of Zang Wenzhong for, according to the rituals, only kings had the right to keep such tortoises.

4 Confucius' disciple.

3.8

子夏问曰："'巧笑倩兮，美目盼兮，素以为绚兮'。何谓也？"

子曰："绘事后素。"

曰："礼后乎？"

子曰："起予者商也，始可与言诗已矣。"

3.12

祭如在，祭神如神在。子曰："吾不与祭，如不祭。"

3.15

子入太庙，每事问。或曰："孰谓鄹（zōu）人之子知礼乎？入太庙，每事问。"子闻之，曰："是礼也。"

14.40

子张曰："《书》云：'高宗谅阴，三年不言。'何谓也？"

子曰："何必高宗？古之人皆然。君薨（hōng），百官总己以听于冢宰三年。"

And when the contest ends, they drink and toast to each other. So they are quite like men of honor when they do contend."

3.8 Zixia asked about the connotation of a verse in the *Book of Songs*. "The pretty dimples of the artful smile, the well-defined black and white of the eyes, are like colorful patterns on plain silk."

The Master answered, "Only when you have a white base, can you paint colors on it."

Zixia said, "Can we then conclude that likewise, regulations and rituals come after humaneness?"

The Master said, "Zixia, you have thrown new light on this verse for me. I can now discuss the *Book of Songs* with you."

3.12 When the Master offered sacrifices to the dead, he did so as if they were present. The same when he offered sacrifices to the gods. The Master said, "If I didn't do so, I might as well not offer any sacrifice."

3.15 When the Master entered the Grand Temple, he asked questions about everything there.

Someone commented, "How can you say the son of that Zou official[1] knows the rituals well? When he entered the temple, he had to ask about everything."

On hearing this, the Master said, "It accords with the rituals to ask questions."

14.40 Zizhang asked, "The *Book of Documents* says, 'King Gao Zong (of Shang Dynasty) remained in mourning for his father, and for three years he did not attend to state affairs.' What does that

1 Referring to Confucius' father, Shuliang Ge

14.41

子曰:“上好礼，则民易使也。”

14.43

原壤夷俟（sì）。子曰:“幼而不孙弟，长而无述焉，老而不死，是为贼。”以杖叩其胫。

14.44

阙党童子将命。或问之曰:“益者与？”

子曰:“吾其居于位也，见其与先生并行也。非求益者也，欲速成者也。”

15.42

师冕见，及阶，子曰:“阶也”。及席，子曰:“席也”。皆坐，子告之曰:“某在斯，某在斯。”

师冕出，子张问曰:“与师言之，道与？”子曰:“然，固相师之道也。”

mean?"

The Master said, "Gao Zong was not the exception. People in ancient times all followed the same rule. When the sovereign passed away, his successor would not attend to state affairs for three years and all the officials would be under the command of the chief minister."

14.41 The Master said, "When those above observe the regulations and rituals, the common people will be easy to command."

14.43 Yuan Xiang sat with his legs spread wide apart. The Master tapped him across the shin with his stick, saying, "You were defiant when you were young and you accomplished nothing when you were grown up. Now that you are old, you still refuse to die. You are what I call a pest."

14.44 A young man from Que Village came to see Confucius as a messenger. Someone asked the Master, "Is he going to make progress?" Confucius answered, "I have seen him take a seat and walk alongside his seniors. What interests him is not how to make progress but how to succeed quickly."[1]

15.42 The blind musician, Mian, called on Confucius. When he reached the steps, the Master said, "Watch your steps." When they came to the mat, the Master said, "Here is the mat."When everyone was seated, the Master told Mian where the different people were seated.

After Mian left, Zizhang asked, "Is that the way to treat a musician?" The Master answered, "Yes, that is the way to help a blind musician."

1 In ancient China, only adults could be seated on a chair. By taking a seat, the young man had violated the rituals. Similarly, he was not supposed to walk alongside his seniors. He should have sat in the corner of the room and walked behind his seniors.

§2.3 “礼”治天下

3.5

子曰:“夷狄之有君，不如诸夏之亡也。”

3.11

或问禘之说，子曰:“不知也。知其说者之于天下也，其如示诸斯乎!”指其掌。

3.13

王孙贾问曰:“与其媚于奥，宁媚于灶，何谓也?”

子曰:“不然。获罪于天，无所祷也。”

3.19

定公问:“君使臣，臣事君，如之何?”

孔子对曰:“君使臣以礼，臣事君以忠。”

4.13

子曰:“能以礼让为国乎，何有? 不能以礼让为国，如礼何?”

6.25

子曰:“觚（gū）不觚，觚哉! 觚哉!”

§ 2.3 Ritual propriety as the basis of good governance.

3.5 The Master said, "Even with a ruler, a culturally backward tribal state[1] is inferior to a state of the central plains without a ruler."

3.11 Someone asked about the theory behind the Di ceremony. The Master answered, "I don't know." And pointing to his palm, he said, "He who knows what it is about may rule all under heaven as easily as placing something here."

3.13 Wangsun Jia[2] asked about the saying "It is better to curry favor with the kitchen god than with Ao[3]."

The Master answered, "That is not so, because if you have offended Heaven, there is no one you can turn to in your prayer."

3.19 Duke Ding of Lu asked, "How should the ruler treat his ministers and how should the ministers serve their ruler?" Confucius answered, "The ruler should treat his ministers according to the rituals while the ministers should serve their ruler with devotion."

4.13 The Master said, "What difficulty can one have if he governs the state by observing regulations and rituals and showing deference to others? If he cannot accomplish this, what use are the regulations and rituals to him?"

6.25 The Master sighed, "A cornered vessel[4] without corners! What cornered vessel is this!"[5]

1 Referring to those in the border areas.

2 A minister of Wei.

3 A god believed to dwell in the southwest coner of a house.

4 It's used for drinking.

5 In ancient times, the sacrificial wine vessel named *Gu* used to be four-cornered. By Confucius' time, it had become round-bottomed. Here, Confucius was complaining about those who had cast away this tradition.

8.2

子曰:“恭而无礼则劳，慎而无礼则葸（xǐ），勇而无礼则乱，直而无礼则绞。君子笃于亲，则民兴于仁；故旧不遗，则民不偷。”

§2.4 “礼”之传承

2.23

子张问:“十世可知也?”

子曰:“殷因于夏礼，所损益可知也；周因于殷礼，所损益可知也。其或继周者，虽百世，可知也。”

3.9

子曰:“夏礼吾能言之，杞不足徵也；殷礼吾能言之，宋不足徵也。文献不足故也。足，则吾能徵之矣。”

3.14

子曰:“周监（jiàn）于二代，郁郁乎文哉！吾从周。”

8.2 The Master said, "Without observing the rituals, courtesy would become tiresome labor, caution would turn to cowardice, courage would lead to disturbance, and straight forwardness to acrimony. When the ruler devotes himself to his parents, the common people will aspire to humaneness. When he does not forsake his friends, his people will not treat each other meanly."

§ 2.4 Continuity of ritual propriety.

2.23 Zizhang asked, "Is it possible for us to know what it will be like ten generations from now?"

The Master answered, "It is possible to know the regulations and rituals which the Shang Dynasty inherited from the Xia Dynasty, including additions and omissions. In the same way, we come to know those which the Zhou Dynasty inherited from the Yin. Therefore, should there be a successor to the Zhou Dynasty, it is also possible to know the regulations and rituals even a hundred generations from now."

3.9 The Master said, "I can discourse on the rituals of the Xia Dynasty, but not on those of Qi (杞)[1] for lack of evidence. Similarly, I can discourse on the rituals of the state of Shang, but not on those of the state of Song[2]. This is because there isn't much documentation on Qi and Song. If there were, I would be able to support what I say with evidence."

3.14 The Master said, "Zhou Dynasty established its own regulations

1 Its people said to be the descendents of Xia.

2 Its people said to be descendents of Shang.

9.3

子曰:“麻冕，礼也；今也纯，俭，吾从众。拜下，礼也；今拜乎上，泰也。虽违众，吾从下。”

and rituals by learning from the two previous dynasties[1]. And how rich its culture! That is why I am for Zhou."

9.3 The Master said, "A hemp cap is what is prescribed by the rituals (when one steps into an ancestral temple). But now, a silk one is used instead. I follow the former practice since it is more economical. To kowtow before ascending the steps (when a minister is received by the sovereign who is seated on a podium) is what is required by the rituals. But now, one kowtows only after having ascended the steps. This is being disrespectful. So, although it is against common practice today, I stick to the old way."

1 Xia and Yin.

三

“乐”“诗”及其与“礼”的关系

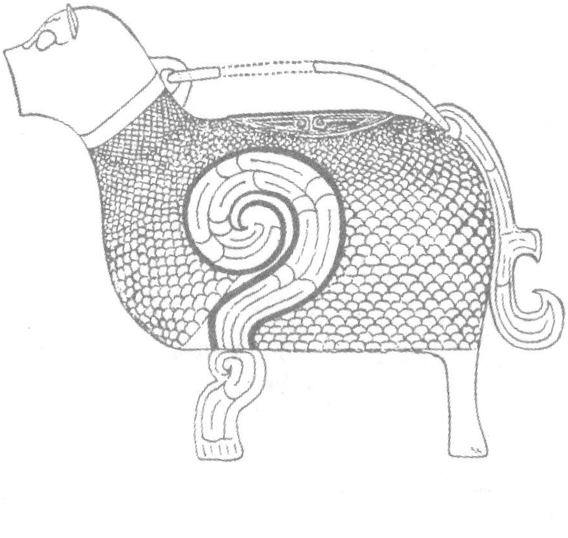

III

Music (乐*yue*) and poetry (诗*shi*) and their relationship with ritual propriety

Confucius on poetry and music

In *The Analects*, Confucius expressed his views about poetry only a few times, yet these comments had a profound influence on traditional Chinese views about literature, both on its forms and content and even its social implications.

As to music, Confucius was infatuated with it because, apart from its entertainment value, it was considered part of the rituals of his time. Music was then closely linked to the occasions when it was performed and even to the social ranks of the listeners.

A performer himself, Confucius had a great respect for the musicians and was well versed in the history of ancient Chinese music. In *The Analects*, there were many passages which show that Confucius was a great lover of music.

There was also a close connection between music and poetry in ancient

2.2

子曰:“《诗》三百,一言以蔽之,曰:‘思无邪。’”

3.20

子曰:“《关雎》,乐而不淫,哀而不伤。”

3.23

子语(yù)鲁大(tài)师乐,曰:“乐其可知也:始作,翕(xī)如也;从(zòng)之,纯如也,皦(jiǎo)如也,绎如也,以成。”

3.25

子谓《韶》:“尽美矣,又尽善也。”谓《武》:“尽美矣,未尽美也。”

7.14

子在齐闻《韶》,三月不知肉味,曰:“不图为乐之至于斯也。”

7.32

子与人歌而善,必使反之,而后和之。

China. Thus, the earliest collection of Chinese poetry which Confucius was fascinated with and frequently quoted in *The Analects* is known as the *Book of Songs*.

2.2 The Master said, "The *Book of Songs* is made up of three hundred poems. They can be summed up in a single phrase, 'a pure heart saturated with unadulterated sentiments.'"

3.20 The Master said, "In *Guanju*[1], there is joy without wantonness, sadness without pain."

3.23 The Master discussed music with the Grand Music Master of Lu, saying, "This much can be said of it. When the piece begins, the different instruments all join in. Then, as it develops, it forms a harmonious melody with distinct rhythm, flowing on until it draws to an end."

3.25 The Master said of the music *Shao*[2], "It is the acme of perfection." Of the music *Wu*[3], he said, "It sounds beautiful enough, but not perfectly good."[4]

7.14 The Master heard the *Shao*[5] when he was in the State of Qi. For several months he did not notice what the meat he ate tasted like. He said, "I had no idea that music could be so wonderful!"

7.32 When the Master sang along with other people and found a good singer among them, he would always have the song sung again and then join in.

---

1 The first poem in the *Book of Songs*.

2 A piece of music passed down from the reign of the ancient king Shun.

3 A piece of music popular during the reign of King Wu of the Zhou Dynasty.

4 Shun inherited his reign peacefully from Yao, whereas King Wu subdued the Ying Dynasty by war. To Confucius, Shun was more virtuous.

5 Ancient music of Shun.

8.8

子曰："兴于诗，立于礼，成于乐。"

8.15

子曰："师挚之始，《关雎》之乱，洋洋乎盈耳哉！"

9.15

子曰："吾自卫反鲁，然后乐正，《雅》《颂》各得其所。"

9.31

"唐棣之华，偏其反而。岂不尔思，室是远而。"子曰：未之思也，夫何远之有？

13.5

子曰："诵《诗》三百，授之以政，不达；使于四方，不能专对。虽多，亦奚以为？"

17.11

子曰："礼云礼云，玉帛云乎哉？乐云乐云，钟鼓云乎哉？"

17.4

子之武城，闻弦歌之声。夫子莞尔而笑，曰："割鸡焉用牛刀？"

8.8 The Master said, "In the *Book of Songs*, one finds inspiration; in rituals, the way to establishment; in music, self- perfection."

8.15 The Master said, "When master musician Zhi of Lu began to play *The Cry of the Osprey*, the music reached a crescendo, and what a flood of wonderful notes filled the ears."

9.15 The Master said, "It was only after my return from Wei to Lu that the music was put in the right order and the *Ya* and the *Sung*[1] were restored to their proper places."

9.31 "The flowers of the *tangti* tree,
How gracefully they dance.
Not that I do not miss you,
It's just that your home is so far away."[2]
The Master commented, "The poet did not really miss her. If he did, her being far away would not have been a problem."

13.5 The Master said, "A person may be able to recite three hundred verses from the *Book of Songs* by heart and yet fails when given administrative responsibilities and proves incapable of using his own initiative when sent as emissary to foreign states. If such is the case, then what use is it for him to recite so much of this book?"

17.11 The Master said, "They talk of the rituals, but surely these are not limited to the ceremonial presentation of jade and silk. They talk of music, but surely it is not limited to the playing of bells and drums."

17.4 The Master went to Wu Cheng (where his student Ziyou was the

1 Sections of the *Book of Songs*.

2 A poem from the *Book of Songs*.

子游对曰:“昔者偃也闻诸夫子曰:‘君子学道则爱人，小人学道则易使也。’”

子曰:“二三子！偃之言是也。前言戏之耳。”

17.9

子曰:“小子何莫学夫《诗》。《诗》，可以兴，可以观，可以群，可以怨。迩之事父，远之事君；多识于鸟兽草木之名。”

17.10

子谓伯鱼曰:“女为《周南》《召南》矣乎？人而不为《周南》《召南》，其犹正墙面而立也与？”

18.9

大师挚适齐，亚饭干适楚，三饭缭适蔡，四饭缺适秦，鼓方叔入于河，播鼗（táo）武入于汉，少师阳、击磬襄入于海。

county magistrate). There he heard the sound of music played on the *Qing* and someone singing. The Master broke into a smile and said, "Surely you don't need an ox-cleaver to kill a chicken."
Ziyou said, "Some time ago, I heard you say: 'When a man of honor is instructed in the Way, he will love his fellowmen; when a petty-minded man is instructed in the Way, it will be easier to command him.'"
The Master said, "My young friends, Ziyou is right. What I just said is merely a joke."

17.9 The Master said, "My young friends, why do none of you study the *Book of Songs*? It will enrich your imagination, enhance your power of observation, help you communicate with people and master the art of expressing grief. It will enable you to better serve your father and even your sovereign. And you will learn the names of many birds and animals, plants and trees."

17.10 The Master said to his son, Bo Yu, "Have you studied *Zhou Nan* and *Zhao Nan*?[1] A man who has not done so will be stonewalled and get nowhere in his life."

18.9 The master musician, Zhi, left for the State of Qi. The musician for the second course, Gan, left for Chu. The musician for the third course, Liao, left for Cai; the musician for the fourth course, Que, left for Qin. The drummer, Fan Shu, went to live in seclusion by the Yellow River. The player of the hand drum, Wu, settled along the Han River. The master musician's deputy, Yang, and player of the chime bells, Xiang, settled by the sea.[2]

---

1 *Zhou Nan* and *Zhao Nan* are the first two chapters of *Guo Feng* in the *Book of Songs*.

2 When the rituals collapsed in the state of Lu and ritual music was abandoned, the musicians each went their own way. In ancient times, the rulers had their meals to the accompaniment of music and each musician would play for a specific course of food. Hence the titles"the musician for the second course", "the musician for the third course", and so on.

四

孔子的其它价值观

IV

Other Confucian Values

§4.1 德

1.7

子夏曰:“贤贤易色;事父母能竭其力;事君,能致其身;与朋友交,言而有信。虽曰未学,吾必谓之学矣。”

§ 4.1 Virtue/Virtuosity (德 *de*).

Confucius on Virtue / Virtuosity (德 *de*)

Confucius believed that the main reason for the political problems during his time — clashes and intrigues in the court and wars between various states — was the lowering of the ethical standards of the rulers and their ministers. Consequently, Confucius reasoned that if the moral standards of the aristocracy could be improved, which in turn would influence the people, then there would be peace among states and improvement in people's lives. Thus, he strongly advocated humane government and virtuous rule. What Confucius proposed in his theory of virtuous rule may be compared to today's meritocracy.

Therefore, Confucius attached great importance to the moral edification of the officials from top to bottom, in both the court and the localities. Many passages in *The Analects* deal with this issue.

And Confucius did not just set the standards for others. To be virtuous in his own conduct was for him a life-long pursuit. "Failure to cultivate virtue and review what I have learned, inability to practice what I have been told to be righteous and unwilling to correct my mistakes — these are what worry me," the Master stressed. (*7.3*)

1.7 Zixia[1] said, "When a man values virtue more than good looks, tries his best to serve his parents, is ready to sacrifice his life for his ruler and keeps his promises with his friends, then I say he is well-educated even if he has not had the benefit of being taught."

1 Confucius' disciple.

9.18

子曰:“吾未见好德如好色者也。”

12.10

子张问崇德辨惑。子曰:“主忠信，徙义，崇德也。爱之欲其生，恶之欲其死，既欲其生，又欲其死，是惑也。‘诚不以富，亦祇以异。’”

13.22

子曰:“南人有言曰:‘人而无恒，不可以作巫医。’善夫!”“不恒其德，或承之羞。”子曰: 不占而已矣。”

14.4

子曰:“有德者必有言，有言者不必有德。仁者必有勇，勇者不必有仁。”

14.5

南宫适问于孔子曰:“羿善射，奡（ào）荡舟，俱不得其死然。禹稷躬稼而有天下。”夫子不答。南宫适出。子曰:“君子哉若人! 尚德哉若人!”

9.18 The Master said, "I have yet to meet a man who loves virtue as much as beauty."

12.10 Zizhang asked how one could cultivate virtue and the ability to resolve doubts at times of confusion. The Master said, "Make it your guiding principle to be loyal and trustworthy and keep to the path of righteousness and you will be cultivating virtue. When you love a person, you want him to have a long life, but when you hate him, you want him to die. When you want him both to live and to die, that is confusion. 'If you did not love her for her riches, you must have forsaken me, for you have changed your mind'[1]."

13.22 The Master said, "There is a saying among the southerners: 'A person who lacks constancy will not make a healer.' How true that is." "If one does not show constancy in virtue, one will someday suffer shame."[2] The Master commented, "For someone like that, there is no point in him consulting the oracle."

14.4 The Master said, "A virtuous man is sure to be eloquent; but an eloquent man is not necessarily virtuous. A humane person is sure to be courageous; but a courageous man is not necessarily humane."

14.5 Nangong Kuo[3] asked Confucius, "Yi was an excellent archer. Ao was skilled in sailing. Both met an untimely death. Yu and Ji, on the other hand, farmed the land. Both won the empire. (What conclusion can one draw from this?)" The Master gave no answer.

---

1 From the *Book of Songs*.

2 From the *Book of Change*.

3 Another name for Nan Rong, Confucius' disciple.

14.33

子曰:“骥不称其力，称其德也。”

14.34

或曰:“以德报怨，何如?”子曰:“何以报德? 以直报怨，以德报德。”

15.4

子曰:“由! 知德者鲜矣。”

15.13

子曰:“已矣乎! 吾未见好德如好色者也。”

17.13

子曰:“乡愿，德之贼也。”

17.14

子曰:“道听而涂说，德之弃也。”

§ 4.2 中庸

After Nangong Kuo had left, the Master said, "What a man of honor he is! How he upholds virtue!"

14.33 The Master said, "A steed which covers a thousand *li* a day is valued not for its strength but for its steadfastness."

14.34 Someone asked, "What do you think of the saying 'Repay injury with a good turn'?" The Master said, "How then are you going to repay a good turn? You repay an injury with justice. You repay a good turn with a good turn."

15.4 The Master said, "Zilu, how few are those who understand virtue!"

15.13 The Master said, "Alas! I have yet to meet a man who loves virtue as he does beauty." (almost similar to passage ***9.18***)

17.13 The Master said, "A person who never says no and seeks to please everybody is the scourge of virtue."

17.14 The Master said, "One who spreads something based on heresay casts virtue to the wind."

§ 4.2 The method of the mean (中庸 *zhongyong*).

Confucius on The Mean (中庸 *zhongyong*)

In *The Analects*, the term "The Mean" appears only once. The Master said, "The Mean embodies the highest form of virtue. Yet it has long been found lacking among the common people." (***6.29***) Still it is an important component of Confucius' philosophy.

Perhaps, this idea of his can be made clearer when we cite some of its

6.29

子曰:“中庸之为德也，其至矣乎！民鲜久矣。”

11.16

子贡问:“师与商也孰贤？”

子曰:“师也过，商也不及。”

曰:“然则师愈与？”子曰:“过犹不及。”

11.22

子路问:“闻斯行诸？”子曰:“有父兄在，如之何其闻斯行之？”

冉有问:“闻斯行诸？”子曰:“闻斯行之。”

公西华曰:“由也问闻斯行诸，子曰，‘有父兄在’；求也问闻斯行诸，子曰，‘闻斯行之’。赤也惑，敢问。”

applications in the same book.

When his disciple Zigong asked the Master how to evaluate two of his fellow disciples, Zizhang and Zixia, Confucius answered, "Zizhang tends to go too far. With Zixia , it is not far enough." Zigong then asked, "Does that make Zizhang better?" The Master answered, "Going too far is just as bad as not going far enough."(***11.16***)

The idea of "The Mean" implies maintaining just the right amount of some quality in one's behavior. It is against one-sidedness, going to extremes and over doing something. It is a methodology permeating in Confucius' ideology.

Readers who are interested in this concept may read the Chinese classic *Zhongyong* (中庸) where it is explained in great detail.

6.29 The Master said, "The Mean (*zhongyong*) embodies the highest form of virtue. Yet it has long been found lacking among the common people."

11.16 Zigong asked, "Who is the better of the two, Zizhang or Zixia?"
The Master said, "Zizhang tends to go too far. With Zixia, it is not far enough."
"Does that make Zizhang better?"
"Going too far is just as bad as not going far enough."

11.22 Zilu asked, "Should I practise at once what I've just learned?"
The Master said, "Your father and elder brothers are still alive, how can you practise what you have just learned?"
When Ranyou asked the same question, the Master said, "Yes, you should."
(Commenting on this,) Gongxi Hua said, "I'm puzzled. They asked the same question, but got two different answers." Confucius said,

子曰：“求也退，故进之；由也兼人，故退之。”

13.21

子曰：“不得中行而与之，必也狂狷（juàn）乎！狂者进取，狷者有所不为也。”

§4.3 和

1.12

有子曰：“礼之用，和为贵。先王之道，斯为美。小大由之，有所不行。知和而和，不以礼节之，亦不可行也。”

"Ranyou usually holds himself back, so I urged him on. Zilu is too bold, so I tried to hold him back."

13.21 The Master said, "If one is unable to associate with those who follow the golden mean, then associate with those with ambition or those who are cautious. The former are enterprising while the latter will draw the line at certain kinds of behavior."

§ 4.3 Harmony (和 *he*)

Confucius on harmony (和 *he*).

In *The Analects*, there were only two passages on the term harmony, yet it is a key concept in Confucius' teachings and can have widespread application today. In our closely connected world, harmonious relations between different countries, ideologies, religions, and among different sects of the same religion, are essential to our very existence. The current wars and clashes which cause so much suffering, so many deaths and destruction, all underline the importance of harmonious relationship to humankind. As Confucius succinctly noted, "Different but harmonious," in human relationship, that is the key to a good life. This was true 2000 years ago, and it is even truer today with our modern inventions, of such great constructive and destructive capabilities.

1.12 Master You said, "In conducting the rituals, the principle of harmony is the most valuable. This was the most important aspect of the Way of the ancient kings. Everything they did,

13.23

子曰，“君子和而不同，小人同而不和。”

§4.4 忠、恕

14.7

子曰：“爱之，能勿劳乎？忠焉，能勿诲乎？”

15.6

子张问行。子曰“言忠信，行笃敬，虽蛮貊之邦，行矣。言不忠信，行不笃敬，虽州里，行乎哉？立则见其参于前也，在舆则见其倚于衡也，夫然后行。”

子张书诸绅。

15.24

子贡问曰：“有一言而可以终身行之者乎？”子曰：“其恕乎！己所不欲，勿施于人。”

great or small, was done according to this rule. However, there is a limit to that. When harmony is sought for its own sake and when it is not regulated by rituals, then the principle will not work."

13.23 The Master said, "A man of honor seeks harmony but not identity of views; a petty-minded man seeks identity but not true harmony."

§ 4.4 Loyalty (忠 *zhong*) and Forbearance (恕 *shu*).

14.7 The Master said, "Should we make no demands on those whom we love? Should we refrain from educating those we are loyal to?"

15.6 Zizhang asked how a man should conduct himself in order to get things done. The Master said, "If you speak with sincerity and trust and behave with honor and reverence, you will get things done even if you are living among backward tribes. However, if you do the contrary, will you get anything done even if you are among your neighbors? Wherever you are, you should keep in mind these moral precepts."

Zizhang had these words written on his sash.

15.24 Zigong asked, "Is there a single word which a person should take as his life-long motto?" The Master answered, "There is, and that word should be 'forbearance'. Do not do unto others what you would not others do unto you."

4.15

子曰:“参乎，吾道一以贯之。”

曾子曰:“唯。”

子出，门人问曰:“何谓也?”

曾子曰:“夫子之道，忠恕而已矣。”

§4.5　信、互信及守信（言而有信）

2.22

子曰:“人而无信，不知其可也。大车无輗（ní），小车无軏（yuè），其何以行之哉?”

§4.6　义

4.15 The Master said, "Cen, there is one thing that pervades my teachings."

Zeng Cen answered, "Yes, indeed."

After the Master had left, the other disciples asked Zeng Cen what Confucius was referring to.

Zeng Cen explained, "The Master simply meant that loyalty and for-bearance form the essence of his teachings."

§ 4.5 Trust (信*xin*), mutual trust among people and being truthful to one's words.

2.22 The Master said, "How can a person get on if he is not trustworthy? It is just like a cart without a collar-bar or a carriage without a yoke-bar. How can he make it move?"

§ 4.6 Justice/Appropriateness/Righteousness (义*yi*).

Confucius on Justice/Appropriateness (义 *yi*)

Confucius noted that "the man of honor thinks in terms of righteousness (义*yi*). The petty man in terms of gains." (***4.16***) He said, "Wealth and prestige acquired not in appropriate ways are to me no more than floating clouds." (***7.16***) However, many commentators have noted that Confucius was not against gains per se. What he was concerned was

1.13

有子曰:“信近于义，言可复也；恭近于礼，远耻辱也；因不失其亲，亦可宗也。”

2.24

子曰:“非其鬼而祭之；谄也。见义不为，无勇也。”

4.10

子曰:“君子之于天下也，无适（dí）也，无莫也，义之与比。”

6.5

原思为之宰，与之粟九百，辞。子曰:“毋，以与尔邻里乡党乎！”

15.17

子曰:“群居终日，言不及义，好行小慧，难矣哉！”

that the gains should be made appropriately and by just means.

1.13 Master You said, "So long as a promise is in line with righteousness (义*yi*), it should be kept. So long as respect conforms with rituals, it will keep humiliation at a distance. It follows that relying on those with whom one has close relationship is dependable."

2.24 The Master said, "It is servility to offer sacrifices to ancestors who are not one's own. It is cowardice not to uphold righteousness when it is called for."

4.10 The Master said, "In dealing with the affairs of the state, there are no set rules as to what should be done or should not be done. Do what is reasonable and appropriate."

6.5 When Yuan Si[1] became Confucius' steward, he was given 900 measures of grain. Yuan Si declined. The Master said, "Don't decline. If you wish, you can give some of it to your neighbors, be they distant or close."

15.17 The Master said, "To mix with a crowd all day, handing out small favors, yet never touching on the subject of justice — such a person is a hopeless case indeed."

1 Confucius' disciple.

§4.7 正名

§ 4.7 Rectification of names (正名 *zhengming*).

Confucius on Rectification of Names (正名 *zhengming*)

Confucius considered it important that names/terms should be used correctly because during his time, people played different roles in society according to their status when observing ritual propriety.

For example, Confucius acted differently in the presence of different-ranking officials and before the Duke of Lu. This included his manners and way of presenting his ideas. Thus, it was important that the people used the right names/terms when speaking to others.

When Duke Jing of Qi asked Confucius about governance, the latter said, "Let the sovereign be a sovereign, the subject be a subject, the father a father and the son a son" (***12.11***). And he was not repeating himself or playing on words. What Confucius was stressing is that the sovereign should act as a sovereign and be treated like a sovereign. In other words, one should be true to his social position.

When his disciple Zilu asked Confucius "Should the Duke of Wei let you administer his state, what is the first thing you would do?", the Master answered, "Use the names correctly."

Elaborating his point, Confucius went on, "If things are not called by their proper names, one's argument cannot stand to reason. If one's argument cannot stand to reason, nothing can be accomplished. If nothing can be accomplished, the regulations and rituals as well as music will not flourish. If these do not flourish, punishment for crime will not be appropriate. If punishment for crime is not appropriate, the common people will have nothing to go by. Thus, when the man of

13.3

子路曰:“卫君待子为政，子将奚先?”

子曰:“必也正名乎!”

子路曰:“有是哉，子之迂也! 奚（xī）其正?”

子曰:“野哉，由也! 君子于其所不知，盖阙如也。名不正则言不顺，言不顺则事不成，事不成则礼乐不兴，礼乐不兴则刑罚不中，刑罚不中，则民无所措手足。故君子名之必可言也，言之必可行也。君子于其言，无所苟而已矣。”

honor uses a name, there must be a reason for it and what he says must be practicable. The man of honor is anything but casual with his words." In today's world, every political party understands Confucius' point and is very careful with its slogans when trying to carry out a national program. Not only must these slogans be attractive and inspiring but they must fit in with reality and be practicable.

13.3 Zilu asked, "Should the Duke of Wei let you administer his state, what is the first thing you would do?"

The Master said, "Use the names properly."

Zilu said, "Is that so! Aren't you being pedantic? Why must the names be used properly?"

The Master said, "How boorish you are! A man of honor would never offer an opinion on something he has no knowledge of. If things are not called by their proper names, one's argument cannot stand to reason. If one's argument cannot stand to reason, nothing can be accomplished. If nothing can be accomplished, the regulations and rituals as well as music will not flourish; if these do not flourish, punishment for crime will not be appropriate; if punishment for crime is not appropriate, the common people will have nothing to go by. Thus, when the man of honor uses a name, there must be a reason for it and what he says must be practicable. The man of honor is anything but casual with his words."[1]

1 There was an internicine struggle for power in the state of Wei during which both father and son tried to seize the rein. Since the distinctions between their status were blurred, Confucius advocated that the first measure to be taken should be the proper use of names.

§4.8 智

6.23

子曰："知者乐（yào）水，仁者乐山；知者动，仁者静；知者乐，仁者寿。"

12.6

子张问明。子曰："浸润之谮（zèn），肤受之愬（sù），不行焉，可谓明也已矣。浸润之谮，肤受之愬，不行焉，可谓远也已矣。"

15.8

子曰："可与言而不与之言，失人；不可与言而与言，失言。知者不失人，亦不失言。"

15.27

子曰："巧言乱德。小不忍则乱大谋。"

§4.9 孝

§ 4.8 Wisdom (智 *zhi*).

6.23 The Master said, "The wise love the waters, the humane love the mountains. The wise love activity, the humane tranquility. The wise enjoy life; the humane are blessed with longevity."

12.6 Zizhang asked about clear-sightedness. The Master said, "When one is not affected by slanders though they have been assiduously repeated, nor by false charges suddenly thrown at him, he can be said to be clear-sighted. More than that, he can be said to be far-sighted."

15.8 The Master said, "To fail to advise a person who can benefit from it is to let that person go to waste. To advise a person who cannot benefit from it is to let your words go to waste. A wise man will waste neither man nor words."

15.27 The Master said, "Being sweet-tongued is enough to forsake one's virtue. Lack of forbearance in small matters spoils great plans."

§ 4.9 Filial Piety (孝 *xiao*).

Confucius on Filial Piety (孝*xiao*)

Filial piety is a core value in Confucius' ethical system. According to him, the fact that one is born and sustained by one's parents when one is a child makes one feel a natural love for one's parents amd gratitude

1.2

有子曰:“其为人也孝弟，而好犯上者，鲜矣；不好犯上，而好作乱者，未之有也。君子务本，本立而道生。孝弟也者，其为仁之本与?”

1.6

子曰:“弟子入则孝，出则弟，谨而信，汎爱众，而亲仁，行有余力，

towards them. And this bond and relationship last throughout one's life. Thus, it is not enough just to provide for one's parents.They must be treated with love and care. When one's parents are alive, one should not travel to places far away from them. And this bond should extend all the way till the parents' death and after—the observation of mourning for one's lost ones should last as long as three years.

To Confucius and his disciples, filial piety is not limited to one's responsibility towards one own family. It is also the root for fraternal relationship with one's siblings, for friendship with others, and for respecting one's teachers and superiors.

In China, thanks to this traditional value, the feeling of closeness and concern embrace the entire extended family even to this day. In the countryside, especially, one is responsible for the continuation of the family line. During the Chinese Lunar New Year, hundreds of millions of people travel long distances to be home for family reunions. In this respect, it is interesting to note that the tradition of compiling the family tree (家谱) has been revived in many parts of China.

1.2 Master You[1] said, "It is rare for one who is filial to his parents and respectful to his elder brothers to disobey his superiors. It is unheard of that one who would obey his superiors should go about creating trouble or even starting a rebellion. The man of honor devotes his attention to the basics. When he has mastered the basics, he is sure to find the key to the Way (道*dao*). Couldn't we say that fulfilling one's filial and fraternal duties constitute the basics of being humane (仁*ren*)?"

1.6 The Master said, "At home, a young man should be filial to his

1 You Ruo, Confucius' disciple.

则以学文。”

1.11

子曰：“父在，观其志；父没，观其行；三年无改于父之道，可谓孝矣。”

2.5

孟懿子问孝，子曰：“无违。”

樊迟御，子告之曰：“孟孙问孝于我，我对曰无违。”

樊迟曰：“何谓也。”

子曰：“生，事之以礼；死，葬之以礼，祭之以礼。”

2.6

孟武伯问孝，子曰：“父母唯其疾之忧。”

2.7

子游问孝，子曰：“今之孝者，是谓能养。至于犬马，皆能有养，不敬，何以别乎？”

parents. Away from home, he should be respectful to his elders. He should be cautious and be true to his words. He should love his fellowmen and befriend the humane. If he still has energy to spare, let him devote himself to studying *Wen* (文)"[1]

1.11 The Master said, "Observe a person's aspirations when his father is still around, then see how he behaves when his father has passed away. If three years later he still sticks to his father's way, he may be described as filial."[2]

2.5 Meng Yizi[3] asked about filial piety. The Master answered, "Do not go against the rules."

Later, when Fan Chi[4] was driving a carriage for him, the Master said, "Meng Yizi asked what being filial meant and I answered, 'Do not go against the rules.'"

"What did you mean by that?" asked Fan.

To which the Master answered, "When your parents are alive, serve them according to the rituals; when they pass away, bury and offer sacrifices to them according to the rituals, too."

2.6 Meng Wubo[5] asked about filial piety. The Master replied, "Let your parents have no cause for worry other than your health."

2.7 Ziyou asked about filial piety. The Master answered, "Nowadays, one is praised as a filial son because he is able to provide for his parents. However, he also provides for his dogs and horses.

---

1 The study of historical documents and the six arts, i.e. rites, music, archery, charioting, writing and arithmetic.

2 The custom at Confucius' time required people to stay at home for three years after the death of their parents.

3 A minister of the state of Lu.

4 Confucius' disciple.

5 Son of Meng Yizi.

2.8

子夏问孝，子曰：“色难。有事，弟子服其劳；有酒食，先生馔，曾是以为孝乎？”

2.24

子曰：“非其鬼而祭之；谄也。见义不为，无勇也。”

3.26

子曰：“居上不宽，为礼不敬，临丧不哀，吾何以观之哉？”

4.18

子曰：“事父母几（jī）谏，见志不从，又敬不违，劳而不怨。”

4.19

子曰：“父母在，不远游，游必有方。”

4.20

子曰：“三年无改于父之道，可谓孝矣。”

4.21

子曰：“父母之年，不可不知也。一则以喜，一则以惧。”

Where is the difference, then, if the son does not treat his parents with respect?"

2.8 Zixia asked about filial piety. The Master answered, "The difficulty lies in having the right feeling. Whether one consistently serves his parents with enthusiasm makes a big difference. If the son does nothing more than helping his parents when there is work to be done and sharing with them when food and drink are available, that alone can hardly be described as being filial."

2.24 The Master said, "It is servility to offer sacrifices to ancestors who are not one's own. It is cowardice not to uphold righteousness when it is called for."

3.26 The Master said, "I cannot put up with a person who, while in high position, is lacking in tolerance, and who shows no reverence while performing the rituals and feels no grief while in mourning."

4.18 The Master said, "When serving your parents, be gentle when you try to dissuade them from doing wrong. Should your advice be ignored, remain reverent and obedient. Do not feel bitter even though laden with anxiety."

4.19 The Master said, "Do not travel to distant places when your parents are alive. If you have to do so, always let them know where you are."

4.20 The Master said, "You can be considered truly filial if you stick to your father's ways for three years after his death." (The same passage appeared in ***1.11***)

4.21 The Master said, "You must not ignore your parents' growing age, for it is something both to rejoice over and to be anxious

8.3

曾子有疾，召门弟子曰："启予足！启予手！《诗》云：'战战兢兢，如临深渊，如履薄冰。'而今而后，吾知免夫，小子！"

13.18

叶公语孔子曰："吾党有直躬者，其父攘羊，而子证之。"

孔子曰："吾党之直者异于是：父为子隐，子为父隐，直在其中矣。"

17.21

宰我问："三年之丧，期（jī）已久矣。君子三年不为礼，礼必坏；三年不为乐，乐必崩。旧谷既没，新谷既升，钻燧改火，期可已矣。"

子曰："食夫稻，衣夫锦，于女安乎？"

曰："安。"

"女安则为之。夫君子之居丧，食旨不甘，闻乐不乐，居处不安，故不为也。今女安，则为之！"

宰我出，子曰："予之不仁也！子生三年，然后免于父母之怀，夫三年之丧，天下之通丧也。予也有三年之爱于其父母乎？"

about."

8.3 Master Zeng was ill. He summoned his disciples and said to them, "Look at my feet and look at my hands. The *Book of Songs* says, 'trembling and shaking as if approaching a deep abyss, as if walking on thin ice.'[1] I know I am spared of trouble. Take care, young friends!"

13.18 The Governor of She said to Confucius, "In my village there is an upright man who reported his father to the authorities for stealing a sheep."

Confucius said, "In my village, those who are upright are quite different. Fathers cover up for their sons, and sons cover up for their fathers. That is one example of being upright."[2]

17.21 Zaiwo said, "Three years is much too long for anyone to be in mourning for one's parents. If the man of honor does not practise the rituals for three years, they will surely be forgotten. If he does not play the music for three years, it will lose its tune. After the supply of old grain is exhausted and the new grain is in, and a new fire has been lit for the new year, that should be sufficient for the mourning period."

The Master asked, "Would you be at ease eating fine rice and wearing silk dresses during the three years' mourning?"

"Yes, I would," Zaiwo answered.

The Master said, "If you can be at ease doing all that, do as you please. A man of honor in mourning does not relish eating delicious food. He finds no pleasure in listening to music, nor

1 This quote from the *Book of Songs* was aimed at showing that one's body belonged to his parents and must be preserved as a sign of filial piety.

2 Confucius' ethics is based on the principle of paternal love and filial piety.

§4.10 志

9.26

子曰:“三军可夺帅也，匹夫不可夺志也。”

9.28

子曰:“岁寒，然后知松柏之后彫也。”

§4.11 勇

9.29

子曰:“知者不惑，仁者不忧，勇者不惧。”

comfort in his own home. That is why he has desisted from doing so. Since you seem to enjoy them, you might as well do what you please."
After Zaiwo left, the Master said, "How inhumane Zaiwo is. A child ceases to be nursed by his parents only after he is three years old. People everywhere under Heaven observe the custom of three years' mourning. Didn't Zaiwo enjoy three years of love and care from his parents?"

§ 4.10 Aspiration (志 *zhi*).

9.26 The Master said, "You can deprive an army of its commanding officer, but you cannot deprive a man of his aspirations."

9.28 The Master said, "Only in the cold of winter is the point brought home that pines and cypresses are the last to fade."

§ 4.11 Bravery (勇 *yong*).

9.29 The Master said, "The wise are not perplexed, the humane do not worry and the brave have no fear."

五

“友”及待人接物之道

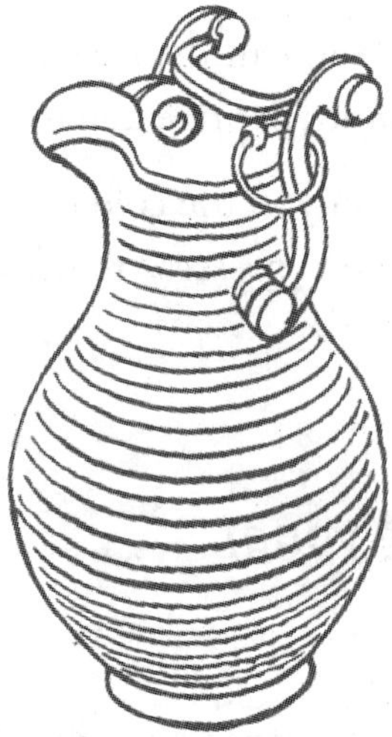

V

On friendship (友 *you*) and the right way to conduct oneself and deal with others

1.16

子曰:“不患人之不己知,患不知人也。”

4.12

子曰:“放于利而行,多怨。”

4.14

子曰:“不患无位,患所以立;不患莫己知,求为可知也。”

4.17

子曰:“见贤思齐焉,见不贤而内自省也。”

4.26

子游曰:“事君数(shuò),斯辱矣;朋友数,斯疏矣。”

5.23

子曰:“伯夷叔齐不念旧恶,怨是用希。”

9.24

子曰:“法语之言,能无从乎?改之为贵。巽与之言,能无说乎?绎之为贵。说(yuè)而不绎,从而不改,吾末如之何也已矣。”

9.25

子曰:“主忠信,毋友不如己者,过则勿惮改。”

1.16 The Master said, "Do not worry about not being appreciated by others. Rather, worry about your not being able to appreciate them."

4.12 The Master said, "He who allows himself to be motivated only by self- interest will incur much ill will."

4.14 The Master said, "Do not worry about not having an official position. Worry about whether you are qualified for such a position. Do not worry when others don't appreciate your work. Rather, try to be worthy of being appreciated."

4.17 The Master said, "When you meet a man of virtue, think how you can become his equal; when you meet a man without virtue, examine yourself to see if you are the same.

4.26 Ziyou said, "Humiliation awaits those who insist on remonstrating with their rulers even when their advice has been rejected. Estrangement awaits those who insist on admonishing their friends even when their advice is not welcome."

5.23 The Master said, "The brothers Bo Yi and Shu Qi bore no grudges against others for their past wrongs and that's why they incurred little ill will."

9.24 The Master said, "How can one not heed the serious and earnest words of criticism uttered by others? What is important is that he corrects himself. How can one not be pleased when he hears agreeable words? What is important is that he analyzes what has been said. I can do nothing with those who are pleased with what others say, but do not analyze, or who agree with everything being said, but do not correct themselves."

9.25 The Master said, "Make it your primary principle to be faithful

12.23

子贡问友。子曰:“忠告而善道之，不可则止，毋自辱也。”

12.24

曾子曰:“君子以文会友，以友辅仁。”

13.24

子贡问曰:“乡人皆好之，何如?”

子曰:“未可也。”

“乡人皆恶之，何如?”

子曰:“未可也。不如乡人之善者好之，其不善者恶之。”

14.20

子曰:“其言之不怍(zuò)，则为之也难。”

14.30

子曰:“不患人之不己知，患其不能也。”

14.31

子曰:“不逆诈，不亿不信，抑亦先觉者，是贤乎!”

15.12

子曰:“人无远虑，必有近忧。”

and trustworthy. Do not accept as friends those whose moral quality is inferior to your own. When you make a mistake, do not be afraid to correct it."

12.23 Zigong asked how one should treat his friends. The Master said, "Advise them in earnest and guide them tactfully, but if they refuse to listen, stop right there and do not lend yourself to rebuff."

12.24 Master Zeng said, "A man of honor makes friends through his learning and looks to friends for support in cultivating humaneness."

13.24 Zigong asked, "What do you think of a person who is liked by everyone in the village?"

The Master said, "That is not enough."

"What do you think of a person who is disliked by everyone in the village?"

"Not enough, either. It would be best if all the good people in his village liked him and all the bad people in his village disliked him."

14.20 The Master said, "He who speaks immodestly will find it hard to live up to his words."

14.30 The Master said, "Worry not about others failing to appreciate you, worry about your own failings."

14.31 The Master said, "He who, without suspecting others or doubting his own credibility, is the first to be aware when others deceive him can be said to be a truly sagacious man."

15.12 The Master said, "Sorrow awaits those who don't take a long view."

15.15

子曰:“躬自厚而薄责于人，则远怨矣。”

15.16

子曰:“不曰‘如之何，如之何’者，吾末如之何也已矣。”

15.28

子曰:“众恶之，必察焉；众好之，必察焉。”

15.41

子曰:“辞达而已矣。”

16.4

孔子曰:“益者三友，损者三友。友直，友谅，友多闻，益矣。友便辟，友善柔，友便佞，损矣。”

15.15 The Master said, "Require much of yourself and little of others, and you will stay away from ill will."

15.16 The Master said, "With those who never ask themselves, 'What should I do? What should I do?', I really don't know what I should do with them."

15.28 The Master said, "Be sure to look into a person's case when everyone dislikes him. The same when everyone seems to like him."

15.41 The Master said, "Words are good enough as long as they can help get your ideas across."

16.4 Confucius said, "It is beneficial to make friends with three types of people: the upright, the trustworthy and the well-informed. It is harmful to make friends with three other types: the obsequious, the double-faced and the smooth-tongued."

六

哲理之言

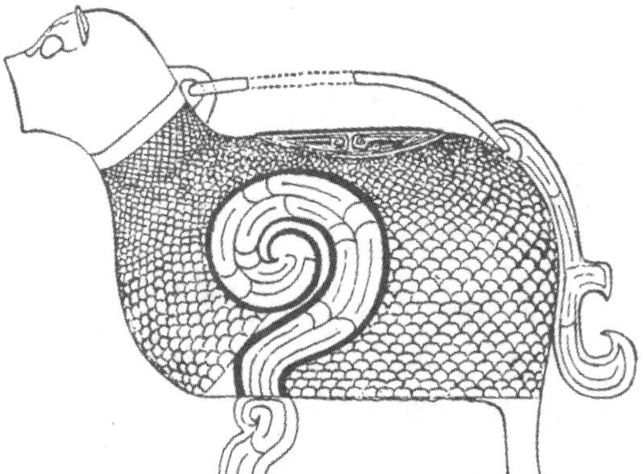

VI

Comments on Philosophical Issues

§6.1　道

4.8

子曰:“朝闻道，夕死可矣。”

5.13

子贡曰:“夫子之文章，可得而闻也；夫子之言性与天道，不可得而闻也。”

6.17

子曰:“谁能出不由户，何莫由斯道也？”

6.24

子曰:“齐一变，至于鲁；鲁一变，至于道。”

8.13

子曰:“笃信好学，守死善道，危邦不入，乱邦不居。天下有道则见(xiàn)，无道则隐。邦有道，贫且贱焉，耻也；邦无道，富且贵焉，耻也。”

9.30

子曰:“可与共学，未可与适道；可与适道，未可与立；可与立，未可与权。”

§ 6.1 The Way (道 *dao*)

The true way of life and nature. By implication, Dao also denotes good governance.

4.8 The Master said, "If in the morning I have learned the Way, I would have no regret dying that same evening."

5.13 Zigong said, "We have heard the Master talk about his views on ancient documents, but seldome about human nature and the Way of Heaven."

6.17 The Master said, "Who can get out of a house but by a door? How is it then that no one is following the Way?"

6.24 The Master said, "With reform, the State of Qi can equal Lu; with reform, Lu can attain the Way."[1]

8.13 The Master said, "Stick to the love of learning and abide by the Way till death. Do not enter a state which is unstable and do not live in a state which is in turmoil. Be visible when the Way prevails. Be invisible when it does not. It is shameful to be poor and humble when the Way prevails. It is equally shameful to be prosperous and in high position when the Way does not prevail."

9.30 The Master said, "A companion in study may not be a companion in the pursuit of the Way. A companion in the pursuit of the Way may not share your stand. And he who shares your stand may not share your moral discretion."

---

1 Lu, whose first duke being the son of Duke Zhou, was considered by Confucius as the model of Duke Zhou's tradition.

14.3

子曰:“邦有道，危言危行；邦无道，危行言孙。”

15.29

子曰:“人能弘道，非道弘人。”

15.40

子曰:“道不同，不相为谋。”

16.2

孔子曰:“天下有道，则礼乐征伐自天子出；天下无道，则礼乐征伐自诸侯出。自诸侯出，盖十世希不失矣；自大夫出，五世希不失矣；陪臣执国命，三世希不失矣。天下有道，则政不在大夫。天下有道，则庶人不议。”

14.3 The Master said, "When the Way prevails in a state, act in an upright way and speak boldly. When the Way does not prevail, act in an upright way but speak with caution."

15.29 The Master said, "Man can enlarge the Way. The Way cannot enlarge man."

15.40 The Master said, "People who have different ideas about the Way need not consult each other."

16.2 Confucius said, "When the Way prevails throughout the land, the Son of Heaven[1] has the final say on major issues like the rituals, music and military expenditures. When the Way does not prevail throughout the land, the sovereigns (of the various states) have the final say on such matters. When they have the final say, their rule will last no more than ten generations. When these prerogatives fall into the hands of their ministers, their rule will last no more than five generations. When these prerogatives fall into the hands of still lower officials, their rule will last no more than three generations. Thus, when the Way prevails throughout the land, decision-making does not rest with the ministers, nor do the common people ever comment on such matters."

1 The king of Zhou.

§6.2 生死 / 时间

9.17

子在川上曰："逝者如斯夫，不舍昼夜。"

9.23

子曰："后生可畏，焉知来者之不如今也？四十、五十而无闻焉，斯

§ 6.2 Life and Death/ Time.

Confucius on Life and Death

Confucius had a very pragmatic mind. What concerned him was how one could make a difference in his lifetime, not what happened to him after his death.

Thus, when his disciple Zilu asked about serving the ghosts and spirits, Confucius answered, "Why should one worry about serving the ghosts and spirits if he is not able to serve the living?" Zilu then asked about death, to which Confucius answered, "How can one understand death if he doesn't even understand life." (*11.12*)

Confucius followed the practice of his time when attending service to the departed. His attitude towards this issue can be understood when another of his quotes is cited.

"Give the common people what is their due, respect the ghosts and spirits but keep a distance from them — that is wisdom."

Confucius knew little about the natural world, and he acknowledged his ignorance, which should be understandable considering the times he lived in. He therefore devoted his attention to the living and not the dead.

Thus, Confucius' philosophy is this-worldly, and not other-worldly at all.

9.17 Standing by a river, the Master declared, "Thus time flows by, never ceasing day or night."

9.23 The Master said, "The young should be regarded with awe. How

亦不足畏也已。”

11.12

季路问事鬼神。子曰:“未能事人，焉能事鬼?”

曰:“敢问死?”

曰:“未知生，焉知死。”

6.22

樊迟问知。子曰，“务民之义，敬鬼神而远之，可谓知矣。”

问仁。曰:“先难而后获，可谓仁矣。”

§6.3 天、天命

do we know the next generation will not surpass the present? Those who have reached the age of forty or fifty, yet still haven't achieved anything to distinguish themselves, need not be taken seriously."

11.12 Zilu asked about serving the ghosts and spirits. The Master said, "Why should one worry about serving the ghosts and spirits if one is not able to serve the living?" Zilu then asked about death. The Master said, "How can one understand death if he does not even understand life."

6.22 Fan Chi asked about wisdom. Confucius said, "Give to the common people what is their due, respect the ghosts and spirits but keep a distance from them — that is wisdom."
Fan Chi asked about humaneness. The Master said, "The humane thinks first of overcoming the difficulties and then of enjoying the benefits. That is humaneness indeed."

§ 6.3 Heaven (天 *tian*) and Mandate of Heaven (天命 *tianming*).

Confucius on Heaven (天*tian*)

In the Introduction, we have already explained how Confucius' Heaven differs from the Western/Christian usage of the word.

Confucius lived 2,500 years ago, when both natural and social sciences

9.5

子畏于匡，曰:“文王既没，文不在兹乎？天之将丧斯文也，后死者不得与于斯文也；天之未丧斯文也，匡人其如予何？”

14.36

公伯寮愬（sù）子路于季孙。子服景伯以告，曰:“夫子固有惑志于公伯寮，吾力犹能肆诸市朝。”

子曰:“道之将行也与，命也；道之将废也与，命也。公伯寮其如命何！”

were still under-developed. There were many phenomena which could not be explained or predicted. That gave rise to the belief of a supernatural force which decided human fate (天命*tianming*). In this respect, Confucius was no different from his contemporaries.

For instance, Confucius once told his disciple Zigong that he no longer wished to say anything. When the latter complained that it would then leave the disciples nothing to transmit to others, the Master answered, "Has Heaven said anything? Yet the four seasons continue to run their course and the plants and animals keep growing …" (*17.19*) This shows that to Confucius Heaven was a decisive force in nature as well.

What is unique about Confucius is that he believed Heaven had given him the mission to restore the cultural and social heritage of the Zhou Dynasty amidst the confusion and troubles of his time. (*9.5*)

This was repeatedly expressed by Confucius when there were setbacks in his career, making him an indefatigable reformer and teacher throughout his life.

9.5 Trapped in Kuang, the Master said, "After King Wen passed away, has not Zhou's culture been vested in me? If Heaven had intended to destroy it, we latecomers would not have been vested with it. Since Heaven did not intend to have it destroyed, how can the men of Kuang do any harm to me?"

14.36 Gongbo Liao spoke ill of Zilu before Jisun. Zifu Jingbo reported this to Confucius, saying, "My lord has been beguiled by Gongbo Liao, but I still have enough influence to have him killed and his corpse displayed on the market."

The Master said, "It is Heaven's will that decides whether the Way shall prevail or perish. What can Gongbo Liao accomplish

17.19

子曰:“予欲无言。”子贡曰:“子如不言，则小子何述焉?”
子曰:“天何言哉? 四时行焉，百物生焉，天何言哉?”

20.3

孔子曰:“不知命，无以为君子也;不知礼，无以立也;不知信，无以知人也。”

§6.4 神、鬼魂

7.21

子不语怪、力、乱、神。

7.35

子疾病，子路请祷。子曰:“有诸?”
子路对曰:“有之。《诔(lěi)》曰:‘祷尔于上下神祇(qí)。’”
子曰:“丘之祷久矣。”

8.3

曾子有疾，召门弟子曰:“启予足! 启予手! 《诗》云:‘战战兢兢，如临深渊，如履薄冰。’而今而后，吾知免夫，小子!”

in the face of the will of Heaven?"

17.19 The Master said, "I no longer wish to say anything." Zigong said, "But if you don't say anything, what is there for us, your disciples, to transmit to others?" The Master said, "Has Heaven said anything? Yet the four seasons continue to run their course and the plants and animals keep growing. Has Heaven said anything?"

20.3 Confucius said, "He who doesn't know his destiny will never become a man of honor. He who doesn't know the rituals will never become established. He who cannot judge the words of others will never be able to really know those who uttered them"

§ 6.4 Gods and spirits.

7.21 The Master never discussed miracles, the use of force, disorders or spirits.

7.35 The Master was seriously ill. Zilu asked for permission to pray to the God for him. The Master asked, "Was this ever done before?" Zilu answered, "Yes. The 'Prayer' says, 'we pray for you to the gods above and below.'"

The Master said, "In that case, I've been saying my prayers all along[1]."

8.3 Master Zeng was ill. He summoned his disciples and said to them, "Look at my feet and look at my hands! The *Book of Songs*

1 A polite way of expressing displeasure.

11.12

季路问事鬼神。子曰:“未能事人，焉能事鬼?”

曰:“敢问死。”曰:“未知生，焉知死?”

§6.5 人性

5.13

子贡曰:“夫子之文章，可得而闻也夫；子之言性与天道，不可得而闻也。”

17.2

子曰:“性相近也，习相远也。”

says, 'trembling and shaking as if approaching a deep abyss, as if walking on thin ice.'[1] I know I am spared of trouble. Take care, young friends!"

11.12 Zilu asked about serving the ghosts and spirits. The Master said, "Why should one worry about serving the ghosts and spirits when he is not even able to serve the living?"

Zilu went on, "May I ask about death?"

The Master said, "How can one understand death when he doesn't even understand life?"

§ 6.5 Human Nature (人性 *renxin*).

Confucius on Human Nature

There is only one passage in *The Analets* where Confucius dealt with the issue of human nature. What he implied is that human beings are by nature pretty similar. It is their upbringing and education that make them different. Therefore it is very important that they get the right education and make a special effort to improve their morality.

5.13 Zigong said, "We have heard the Master talk about his views on ancient documents, but seldom about human nature and the Way of Heaven."

17.2 The Master said, "What nature puts together, habit separates."

1 This quote from the *Book of Songs* was aimed at showing that one's body belonged to his parents and must be preserved as a sign of filial piety.

七

教与学

VII

Learning (学*xue*) and teaching

Confucius on Learning and Teaching

Learning or study constitutes an important topic in *The Analects* and takes up much of its space.

Confucius' father died when he was only three. His widowed mother had to depend solely on herself to rear him. So, Confucius relied mostly on self-study for his education. He recalled in *The Analects* that he became devoted to studying when he was 15-years old. His diligence while still a young man turned him into a prominent scholar.

Confucius was prune to ask questions. "Learning without reflection will end up in confusion and reflection without learning will end up in peril," he noted. And he stressed the need to learn from people around him. "In the company of others, there must some who can be my teacher. I can always choose to learn from their good qualities and avoid their weak points. "

1.1

子曰:“学而时习之，不亦说乎？有朋自远方来，不亦乐乎？人不知，而不愠，不亦君子乎？”

7.25

子以四教：文、行、忠、信。

§7.1 六艺

3.16

子曰:“射不主皮，为力不同科，古之道也。”

In Confucius' time, knowledge consisted of the six basic arts (六艺), i.e. rituals, music, archery, charioting, writing and arithmetic. On a higher level, it also included knowledge of *Yi-Jing, The Book of Songs* and other classics.

Thus, to Confucius, learning was not limited to seeking knowledge, but also included moral cultivation and the ability to handle interpersonal relations. This would include what we term today in China as "quality education" – i.e. moral, intellectual, physical, aesthetic and civic education so that the recipient will be a qualified member of the society.

Confucius also had many good ideas about teaching, which are dealt with under the heading "Confucius, the educationist."

1.1 The Master said, "Is it not a great pleasure to be able to practice frequently what you have learned? Is it not a real delight to have friends come to visit you from afar? Is it not the mark of a man of honor (君子 *junzi*) to not take offence when others fail to appreciate your worth?"

7.25 The Master taught four disciplines: historical documents, social conduct, loyalty to superiors and faithfulness to friends.

§ 7.1 Learning the "six arts (六艺*liuyi*)".

3.16 The Master said, "In archery, the point is not to pierce the hide but to hit the target, for people differ in strength. That was a rule followed by the ancients."

16.5

孔子曰:“益者三乐,损者三乐。乐节礼乐,乐道人之善,乐多贤友,益矣。乐骄乐,乐佚游,乐晏乐,损矣。”

17.22

子曰:“饱食终日,无所用心,难矣哉!不有博奕者乎?为之,犹贤乎已。”

§7.2 自学自强(提升德行)

1.4

曾子曰:“吾日三省吾身:为人谋而不忠乎?与朋友交而不信乎?传不习乎?”

4.6

子曰:“我未见好仁者,恶不仁者。好仁者,无以尚之;恶不仁者,其为仁矣,不使不仁者加乎其身。有能一日用其力于仁矣乎?我未见力不足者。盖有之矣,我未之见也。”

4.14

子曰:“不患无位,患所以立;不患莫己知,求为可知也。”

16.5 Confucius said, "There are beneficial and harmful pleasures. To be restrained by music and rituals, to praise other people's virtues and to befriend worthy people — these are beneficial pleasures. To be soothed by licentious sounds, to idle away time and to indulge in banqueting — these are harmful pleasures."

17.22 The Master said, "It is really intolerable for a person who has a full stomach not to use his brain all day. Why can't he play chess? Even that is better than being idle."

§ 7.2 Learning for self-improvement (striving to improve one's moral character).

1.4 Master Zeng[1] said, "More than once do I examine myself everyday. Have I done my very best to help others? Have I been faithful to my friends? And have I practiced what my master has taught me?"

4.6 The Master said, "I have yet to meet a man who truly loves humaneness, or a person who detests another because he lacks humaneness. He who detests those lacking in humaneness feels so because he does not want to be contaminated by what is inhumane. Is there anyone who can achieve humaneness through his efforts in a single day? I have never seen anyone who has that capacity. Perhaps there are, but I have yet to see one like that."

4.14 The Master said, "Do not worry about not having an official

1 Zeng Cen, Confucius' disciple.

4.17

子曰:“见贤思齐焉，见不贤而内自省也。”

5.27

子曰:“已矣乎，吾未见能见其过而内自讼者也。”

8.5

曾子曰:“以能问于不能，以多问于寡;有若无，实若虚；犯而不校(jiào)，昔者吾友尝从事于斯矣！”

§7.3 学习之道

2.11

子曰:“温故而知新，可以为师矣。”

2.15

子曰:“学而不思则罔，思而不学则殆。”

2.16

子曰:“攻乎异端，斯害也已。”

2.17

子曰:“由！诲女知之乎？知之为知之，不知为不知，是知也。”

position. Worry about whether you are qualified for such a position. Do not worry when others don't appreciate your work. Rather, try to be worthy of being appreciated."

4.17 The Master said, "When you meet a man of virtue, think how you can become his equal; when you meet a man without virtue, examine yourself to see if you are the same."

5.27 The Master said, "Alas! I have yet to find a man who is able to perceive his own errors and criticize himself for them."

8.5 Master Zeng said, "I had a friend who pursued this rule of conduct: to be capable and yet ask for advice from the less capable; to be knowledgeable and yet consult the less knowledgeable; to have and yet seem to lack; to be full and yet seem to be empty; to be offended and yet not to mind."

§ 7.3 Method of learning.

2.11 The Master said, "He who is able to acquire new ideas while reviewing old knowledge is worthy of being a teacher."

2.15 The Master said, "Learning without reflection will end up in confusion; reflection without learning will end up in peril."

2.16 The Master said, "Attacking erroneous ideas will put an end to the harm they have caused."

2.17 The Master said, "Zilu[1], shall I tell you what true knowledge is? Say you know when you know, and say you don't know when

1 Confucius' disciple.

5.9

子谓子贡曰：“女与回也孰愈？”

对曰：“赐也何敢望回？回也闻一以知十，赐也闻一以知二。”

子曰：“弗如也。吾与女弗如也。”

§7.4 教学之心

6.20

子曰：“知之者不如好之者，好之者不如乐之者。”

7.2

子曰：“默而识之，学而不厌，诲人不倦，何有于我哉？”

7.29

互乡难与言，童子见，门人惑。子曰：“与其进也，不与其退也，唯何甚？人洁己以进，与其洁也，不保其往也。”

8.17

子曰：“学如不及，犹恐失之。”

9.19

子曰：“譬如为山，未成一篑，止，吾止也。

you don't, that is true knowledge."

5.9 The Master asked Zigong, "Who is wiser? You or Yan Hui?"
Zigong answered, "How dare I compare myself with Yan Hui? When he is taught one thing, he understands ten. When I am taught one thing, I understand two."
The Master said, "Indeed, you and I are no match for Yan Hui."

§ 7.4 Attitude of learning and teaching.

6.20 The Master said, "To enjoy knowledge is better than to acquire knowledge. To love knowledge is better than both."

7.2 The Master said, "To remember what I have learned, to study hard and never feel contented, to teach others tirelessly, which of these goals are beyond me?"

7.29 People of Huxian were difficult to communicate with.[1] When a boy from that region came and was received by Confucius, his disciples were puzzled. The Master said, "What I approve of is his progress, not his backwardness. Why be so exacting? When a person makes an effort to become a better person, I welcome his progress although I cannot vouch for his past."

8.17 The Master said, "Study as if you might not reach your objective and as if you might forget what you have learned."

9.19 The Master said, "It's like building a mound. If I stopped before the last basket of earth, I would never complete the job. It's like

1 Because they spoke a strange dialect.

譬如平地，虽覆一篑，进，吾往也。

9.22

子曰："苗而不秀者有矣夫！秀而不实者有矣夫！"

14.24

子曰："古之学者为己，今之学者为人。"

15.30

子曰："过而不改，是谓过矣。"

15.31

子曰："吾尝终日不食，终夜不寝，以思，无益，不如学也。"

16.9

孔子曰："生而知之者，上也；学而知之者，次也；困而学之，又其次也；困而不学，民斯为下矣。"

17.8

子曰："由也，女闻六言六蔽矣乎？"

对曰："未也。"

"居，吾语女。好仁不好学，其蔽也愚；好知不好学，其蔽也荡；好信不好学，其蔽也贼；好直不好学，其蔽也绞；好勇不好学，其蔽也乱；好刚不好学，其蔽也狂。"

filling a hollow. Even if I have tipped in only the first basketful of earth, it would be a step forward if I kept at it."

9.22 The Master said, "There are saplings that fail to blossom and saplings that blossom but fail to bear fruit."

14.24 The Master said, "In the past, people studied to improve themselves. Nowadays, they study to impress others."

15.30 The Master said, "A mistake not corrected is a mistake indeed."

15.31 The Master said, "Occupied with thinking, I once spent days without eating and nights without sleep. My efforts turned out to be fruitless. I should have spent the time learning."

16.9 Confucius said, "Those who have innate knowledge are at the top of the scale. Those who study and learn come next. Those who study when faced with difficulties are lower still. Those common people who do not study even when faced with difficulties are the lowest."

17.8 The Master said, "Zilu, have you heard of the six qualities and their accompanying faults?"

"No, I have not."

Confucius said, "Sit down and I will tell you. To love humaneness but not learning may lead to foolishness. To love wisdom but not learning may lead to disorientation. To love good faith but not learning may lead you astray. To love forthrightness but not learning may lead to intolerance. To love courage but not learning may lead to insubordination. To love steadfastness but not learning may lead to recklessness."

§7.5 授业之道

6.21

子曰:“中人以上，可以语上也；中人以下，不可以语上也。”

§ 7.5 Method of teaching.

Confucius, the Educationist

Confucius is remembered today as a leading educationist of ancient China. He was one of the earliest teachers who took in students of lower social strata when education was the sole preserve of children of the aristocracy.

In *The Analects*, there are numerous passages where Confucius expounded his ideas on learning and teaching.

For example, Confucius stressed the importance of thinking and reasoning in the process of learning. Thus, the stress on rote learning, for which the Chinese education system is often subject to criticism, should not be attributed to Confucius. Rather, it is the imperial examination system which caused it. The present stress of innovation should be linked with the need for creative thinking – analysis, synthesis, ability to form new ideas and solve new problems.

To Confucius, learning is not limited to gathering knowledge alone. It is equally if not more important for learning to handle human relations, to be responsible to one's family and society and become an ethical person.

Confucius paid great attention to the unique qualities of his disciples and offered different advices and answers to different students. Thus he was able to provide a type of education unique in his times.

6.21 The Master said, "You can discuss profundity only with those above average, but not with those below average."

7.8

子曰:“不愤不启，不悱不发。举一隅不以三隅反，则不复也。”

§7.6 一视同仁

7.7

子曰:“自行束脩（xiū）以上，吾未尝无诲焉。”

15.39

子曰:“有教无类。”

7.8 The Master said, "I do not try to enlighten my disciples until they have tried hard but failed to understand something. I do not supply my disciples with any new vocabulary or put their ideas into words for them unless they have difficulty doing so. When I have given them one instance and they cannot draw inferences from it, I do not repeat my lesson."

§ 7.6 No discrimination in student admission.

7.7 The Master said, "I have never refused to teach any disciple who offered me ten strips of dried meat[1]."

15.39 The Master said, "In teaching, I take disciples of all background without discrimination."

1 In ancient China, ten strips of dried meat was a common gift presented on one's first visit to a teacher's home.

八

政 *zheng*

VIII

Governance

Confucius on Governance

Governance is an important aspect of Confucian thought. Living in an age of internal strife and wars among dukedoms, Confucius gave much thought to this question and developed his own ideas about good governance.

He had many audiences with the Duke of Lu and his chief ministers where he introduced his ideas and tried to convince them of their efficacy. He had much success as a county head. Then he was appointed minister of justice and had a chance to put his program to practice. According to his advice, the chief ministers were to abolish the fortresses built and controlled by their stewards. This reform process went smoothly until the most powerful chief minister woke up to Confucius' real intentions and abruptly withdrew support. Thus, Confucius' plan to restore power to the Duke came to naught.

Later, when the Duke of Lu and his chief ministers all neglected state

8.9

子曰:“民可使由之,不可使知之。”

12.7

子贡问政,子曰:“足食,足兵,民信之矣。”

子贡曰:“必不得已而去,于斯三者何先?”

曰:“去兵。”

子贡曰:“必不得已而去,于期二者何先?”

曰:“去食。自古皆有死,民无信不立。”

affairs so as to attend the performances of the singsong girls sent by the Duke of the neighboring State of Qi, Confucius realized that his political future in the State of Lu had evaporated.

Thus began his fourteen years of migration to Wei, Song, Chen, Cai and other nearby states where he continued to propagate his ideas about governance, but without success.

Confucius' ideas on governance are varied, but what constitutes its mainstay can be listed as follows: the stress on humaneness and virtuosity, attention to people's welfare, the need to educate the people and emphasis on importance of the exemplary role of government officials. For instance, Confucius stressed that mere punishment alone could only frighten people away from committing crime whereas education can make them not to have crime-committing desires in the first place.

8.9 The Master said, "One can make the common people follow a course of action, but must not let them understand why they should do so."

12.7 Zigong asked about government. The Master said, "The essentials of good government are abundance of food, plenty of arms and the trust of the people."

Zigong asked, "What if one of these three essentials had to be dispensed with, which one should it be?"

The Master said, "Arms."

"What if one of the remaining two had to be dispensed with, which one should it be?"

"Food,"said the Master. "After all, since the beginning of time, no one has been able to escape the fate of death. But without the trust of the common people, the government would have

12.9

哀公问于有若曰:“年饥，用不足，如之何?”

有若对曰:“盍彻乎?”

曰:“二，吾犹不足，如之何其彻也?”

对曰:“百姓足，君孰与不足?百姓不足，君孰与足?”

12.11

齐景公问政于孔子。孔子对曰:“君君、臣臣、父父、子子。”

公曰:“善哉!信如君不君，臣不臣，父不父，子不子，虽有粟，吾得而食诸?”

12.13

子曰:“听讼，吾犹人也。必也使无讼乎。”

12.14

子张问政。子曰:“居之无倦，行之以忠。”

15.33

子曰:“知及之，仁不能守之，虽得之，必失之。知及之，仁能守之，不庄以莅(lì)之，则民不敬。知及之，仁能守之，庄以涖之，动之不以礼，未善也。”

nothing to sustain itself."

12.9 Duke Ai (of Lu) asked Youruo, "We have had a poor harvest and I have not enough to cover my expenditures. What should I do?"

Youruo answered, "Why not introduce a tithe?" The Duke said, "I don't have enough to spend even if I double the rate, how could a tithe do?"

To which Youruo replied, "When the people have plenty, the sovereign will not be in want; when the people are in want, how can the sovereign have plenty?"

12.11 Duke Jing of Qi asked Confucius about government. Confucius replied, "Let the sovereign be a sovereign, the subject a subject, the father a father, the son a son."

The Duke remarked, "Well said. If the sovereign did not act like a sovereign, the subject not like a subject, the father not like a father and the son not like a son, then even if there were plenty of grain, would I get my share?"

12.13 The Master said, "In settling a lawsuit, I am little different from others. Still I feel it is best to do away with all lawsuits."

12.14 Zizhang asked about government. The Master said, "Never slacken your efforts at your post, show your loyalty when carrying out government orders."

15.33 The Master said, "When a man has enough knowledge to attain office but fails to practice humaneness, even if he is in office, he is bound to lose his post. When a man has enough knowledge to attain office and has followed up by practising humaneness, but fails to govern conscientiously, he will not win the respect

16.6

孔子曰:“侍于君子有三愆(qiān):言未及之而言，谓之躁；言及之而不言，谓之隐，未见颜色而言谓之瞽(gǔ)。”

§8.1 “仁”政

1.5

子曰:“道千乘之国，敬事而信，节用而爱人，使民以时。”

2.1

子曰:“为政以德，譬如北辰，居其所而众星共之。”

of the common people. When a man has enough knowledge to attain office, has followed up with humaneness and has governed conscientiously, but fails to move the people with the spirit of the rituals, he still falls short of perfection."

16.6 Confucius said, "There are three mistakes one has to watch out for when one is in attendance on the ruler. To speak before spoken to is being rash. Not to speak when spoken to is being evasive. To speak without observing the listener's facial expressions is being blind."

§ 8.1 Humaneness as its guiding principle.

1.5 The Master said, "In governing a medium-sized state[1], one should devote himself whole-heartedly to state affairs, abide by his words, avoid excessive expenditure, care for his subor-dinates and use the labor of the common people (民*min*) only during the slack season."[2]

2.1 The Master said, "He who rules the country by virtue can be compared to the Polestar which holds its own with a multitude of stars revolving around it."

1 The Chinese original for "a medium-sized state" was "a state equipped with a thousand chariots", equivalent to a medium-sized state during the Spring and Autumn Period.

2 Throughout ancient Chinese history, rulers had the right to call on the common people to work on public projects without recompense. The common people were mostly farmers. They had to work on the public projects, such as building defenses or digging canals without pay, If they had to fulfil these obligations during sowing or harvesting , their own farms would be neglected.

2.20

季康子问:“使民敬忠以劝,如之何?”

子曰:“临之以庄则敬,孝慈则忠,举善而教不能则劝。”

3.26

子曰:“居上不宽,为礼不敬,临丧不哀,吾何以观之哉?”

13.12

子曰:“如有王者,必世而后仁。”

13.15

定公问:“一言而可以兴邦,有诸?”

孔子对曰:“言不可以若是。其几也。人之言曰:‘为君难,为臣不易。’如知为君之难也,不几乎一言而兴邦乎?”

曰:“一言而丧邦,有诸?”

孔子对曰:“言不可以若是。其几也,人之言曰:‘予无乐乎为君,唯

2.20 Ji Kangzi[1] asked, "What should be done to inculcate in the common people reverence and filial piety and eagerness to do their best?"

The Master replied, "Treat the common people with dignity, and they will treat you with reverence; promote filial piety and humaneness and they will be loyal to you; promote the righteous and instruct the incompetent, and they will eagerly do their best."

3.26 The Master said, "I cannot put up with a person who, while in high position, is lacking in tolerance, and who shows no reverence while performing the rituals and feels no grief while in mourning."

13.12 The Master said, "Even with a good king, it would still require an entire generation for his humane rule to prevail."

13.15 Duke Ding of Lu asked, "Is there a single saying that can lead a state to prosperity?"

Confucius answered, "One cannot interpret it in such a simplistic way. There is a maxim which says 'it is difficult to be a sovereign, nor is it easy to be a minister.' If the sovereign realises how difficult his role is, then won't that be almost a case of a single saying leading the state to prosperity?"

Duke Ding asked, "Is there a single saying that can lead a state to ruin?"

Confucius answered, "One cannot interpret it in such a simplistic way. There is a maxim which says that 'the one and only pleasure in being a sovereign is that nobody dares disobey him.'

1 A minister of Lu.

其言而莫予违也。’如其善而莫之违也，不亦善乎？如不善而莫之违也，不几乎一言而丧邦乎？”

3.16

叶公问政。子曰：“近者悦，远者来。”

20.2

子张问孔子曰：“何如斯可以从政矣？”

子曰：“尊五美，屏四恶，斯可以从政矣。”

子张曰：“何谓五美？”

子曰：“君子惠而不费，劳而不怨，欲而不贪，泰而不骄，威而不猛。”

子张曰：“何谓惠而不费？”

子曰：“因民之所利而利之，斯不亦惠而不费乎？择可劳而劳之，又谁怨？欲仁而得仁，又焉贪？君子无众寡、无大小、无敢慢，斯不亦泰而不骄乎？君子正其衣冠，尊其瞻视，俨然人望而畏之，斯不亦威而不猛乎？”

If what he says is right and no one dares disobey him, isn't that a good thing? But if what he says is wrong and no one dares disobey him, will it not be almost a case of a single saying leading the state to ruin?"

13.16 The Governor of She asked about government. The Master answered, "Make those near you happy and those far away will flock to you."

20.2 Zizhang asked Confucius, "How does one qualify for a government official?"

The Master said, "The qualifications are: Respect the five virtues and spurn the four evils."

"What do you mean by the five virtues?" asked Zizhang.

The Master answered, "The man of honor is generous without excesses. He makes people work without causing them to complain. He is ambitious without being greedy. He is self-possessed without being arrogant. He is awe-inspiring without being fierce."

"What do you mean by being generous without excesses?" asked Zizhang.

The Master answered, "If you let the common people do what is beneficial for them, isn't it being generous without excesses? If you make people work on tasks they are capable of accomplishing, who will complain? If your ambition is to attain humaneness, there would be no place for greediness. The man of honor puts the many on a par with the few, the high on a par with the low and dares not to be negligent, isn't that being self-possessed without being arrogant? The man of honor dresses properly and looks dignified, his solemnity causing fear. Isn't he awe-inspiring without being fierce?"

子张曰:“何谓四恶?”

子曰:“不教而杀,谓之虐;不戒视成,谓之暴;慢令致期,谓之贼;犹之与人也,出纳之吝,谓之有司。”

§8.2 礼制而非刑治

2.3

子曰:“道之以政,齐之以刑,民免而无耻;道之以德,齐之以礼,有耻且格。”

6.2

仲弓问子桑伯子。子曰:“可也,简。”

仲弓曰:“居敬而行简,以临其民,不亦可乎?居简而行简,无乃大简乎?”子曰:“雍之言然。”

Zizhang asked "What do you mean by the four evils then?"
The Master answered, "To impose the death penalty without first educating the people amounts to cruelty. To demand achievement without prior requirements amounts to tyranny. To suddenly impose a deadline on a job without previous warning amounts to theft. To act miserly when it comes to giving amounts to stinginess."

§ 8.2 Rule by virtue rather than rule by punishment.

2.3 The Master said, "Rule the people by decrees and put them into place by punishment and they will know how to stay out of trouble. But they will not have a sense of shame. Let them know the way of virtue and keep them in line with regulations and rituals, then they will not only have a sense of shame when they do wrong, but also know the correct course to take."

6.2 Ran Yong asked about Zisang Bozi[1]. The Master said, "He is quite alright. He is simple in style. He does not bother himself with petty matters."
Ran Yong said, "Isn't simplicity in style, when coupled with conscien-tiousness, a good way of ruling the common people? However, if all one cares about is simplicity, and not just in one's own style, isn't it then carrying simplicity too far?" The Master said, "There is some truth in what you said."

1 Somebody in the state of Lu, his background being unknown.

12.19

季康子问政于孔子曰:“如杀无道,以就有道,何如?”

孔子对曰:“子为政,焉用杀?子欲善而民善矣。君子之德风,小人之德草,草上之风,必偃。”

13.11

子曰:“‘善人为邦百年,亦可以胜残去杀矣。’诚哉,是言也!”

§8.3　君主典范

12.17

季康子问政于孔子。孔子对曰:“政者,正也。子帅以正,孰敢不正?”

12.18

季康子患盗,问于孔子。孔子对曰:“苟子之不欲,虽赏之不窃。”

13.1

子路问政。子曰:“先之劳之。”请益。曰:“无倦。”

12.19 Ji Kangzi asked Confucius about government, "What do you think of killing those who do not follow the Way so as to move the people closer to those who follow the Way?"

Confucius answered, "In governing a state, what need is there for you to kill? If you govern the state well, the common people will naturally become good. The morality of the man of honor is like the wind. That of the petty man is like grass. When there is a wind, the grass is sure to bend in the direction the wind blows."

13.11 The Master said, "How true is the saying that 'when good men have governed a state for a hundred years, then cruelty will have been banished and killings will have disappeared.'"

§ 8.3 Rulers as role-models.

12.17 Ji Kangzi asked Confucius about government. Confucius said, "The word *zheng*[1] is a homonym of the word *zheng*[2]. If you set an example by being upright, who would dare to be otherwise?"

12.18 Ji Kangzi was disturbed by the large number of thieves. He asked Confucius for advice. Confucius said, "If you were not covetous, no one would commit burglary even if they were to be rewarded for doing so."

13.1 Zilu asked about government. The Master said, "Set an example

1 政 government.

2 正 upright.

13.6

子曰:“其身正，不令而行；其身不正，虽令不从。”

13.13

子曰:“苟正其身矣，于从政乎何有？不能正其身，如正人何？”

§ 8.4　知人善用

2.10

子曰:“视其所以，观其所由，察其所安，人焉廋哉？人焉廋哉？

2.19

哀公问曰:“何为则民服？”

孔子对曰:“举直错诸枉，则民服；举枉错诸直，则民不服。”

6.14

子游为武城宰。子曰:“女得人焉尔乎？”

曰:“有澹台灭明者，行不由径，非公事，未尝至于偃之室也。”

yourself and the people will work hard." When asked to elaborate, the Master said, "Never slacken your efforts when carrying out this principle."

13.6 The Master said, "If a ruler is correct in his own behavior, then people will obey him without him giving any orders, but if he misbehaves, people will not obey him even if he issued orders."

13.13 The Master said, "If one is upright himself, he should have no difficulty in governance. If he is not upright, how can he correct others?"

§ 8.4 Importance of selecting the right people as administrators.

2.10 The Master said, "Observe a person's behavior, find out what leads him to behave the way he does and see what he rests content with. If one does that, how can that person still manage to hide his true character? How indeed?"

2.19 Duke Ai of the State of Lu asked, "What should I do so that my people will obey me?" The Master replied, "Your people will do so if you promote the straight over the crooked. They will disobey you if you do the opposite."

6.14 Ziyou became the county head of Wu. The Master asked him, "Have you found any talented people there?"

Ziyou answered, "There is one named Duantai Mieming[1]. He

1 Later to become Confucius' disciple.

8.20

舜有臣五人而天下治。武王曰:“予有乱臣十人。”

孔子曰:“才难，不其然乎？唐虞之际，于斯为盛。有妇人焉，九人而已。三分天下有其二，以服事殷。周之德，其可谓至德也已矣。”

13.2

仲弓为季氏宰，问政。子曰:“先有司，赦小过，举贤才。”

曰:“焉知贤才而举之?”

子曰:“举尔所知，尔所不知，人其舍诸?”

15.14

子曰:“臧文仲其窃位者与？知柳下惠之贤而不与立也。”

never takes shortcuts and he never calls on me at my house except on official business."

8.20 Shun had five ministers and all under Heaven was well governed. King Wu of Zhou said, "I have ten capable ministers."

Confucius commented, "Isn't it true that talents are really hard to find? After Yao and Shun, King Wu possessed the greatest number of talented people, but one of his ministers was a woman[1], so actually he had nine. King Wen[2] had two-thirds of the empire, yet (because of his loyalty, he did not overthrow the Yin / Shang Dynasty) he continued to pay homage to Yin. The virtue displayed by the house of Zhou can be said to have reached the zenith."

13.2 When serving as a steward for the Jisun Family, Zhong Gong asked how he should govern. The Master said, "Set an example for your subordinates; be lenient on minor offenses and promote those who are talented."

Zhong Gong asked, "How does one decide who among so many are talented and should be promoted?"

The Master answered, "Promote those you know are talented. Those who are talented but whom you fail to recognize will not be passed over by others."

15.14 The Master said, "Zang Wenzhong[3] was an irresponsible official. He knew well that Liuxia Hui was a man of wisdom, yet he would not recommend him to an official post."

---

1 The mother of King Wu.

2 The father of King Wu.

3 A minister of Lu.

§8.5 因材施教

13.9

子适卫，冉有仆。子曰:“庶矣哉!”

冉有曰:“既庶矣，又何加焉?”

曰:“富之。”

曰:“既富矣，又何加焉?”

曰:“教之。”

§8.6 其它

2.18

子张学干禄，子曰:“多闻阙疑，慎言其余，则寡尤；多见阙殆，慎行其余，则寡悔。言寡尤，行寡悔，禄在其中矣。”

4.13

子曰:“能以礼让为国乎，何有？不能以礼让为国，如礼何?”

§ 8.5 Significance of providing the right kinds of education for the people.

13.9 When Confucius went to the State of Wei, Ranyou drove the carriage for him. The Master remarked, "What a lot of people they have here!"
Ranyou asked, "What can be done with so many people?"
The Master said, "Help them prosper."
Ranyou asked, "When they have become prosperous, then what?"
The Master said, "Educate them."

§ 8.6 Other requirements.

2.18 Zizhang[1] asked the Master how to be an official. The Master replied, "Listen to all kinds of opinions, set aside what is dubious and speak discreetly on the rest. That way, you will make few mistakes. Open your eyes wide, set aside what is dubious and act on the rest with caution. You will then have few regrets. Since a good official makes few mistakes, his success is ensured."

4.13 The Master said, "What difficulty can one have if he governs the state by observing regulations and rituals and showing deference to others? If he cannot accomplish this, what use are the regulations and rituals to him?"

1 Confucius' disciple.

8.14

子曰:“不在其位，不谋其政。”

13.5

子曰:“诵《诗》三百，授之以政，不达；使于四方，不能专对。虽多，亦奚以为？”

13.17

子夏为莒（**jǔ**）父宰，问政。子曰:“无欲速，无见小利。欲速则不达，见小利则大事不成。”

14.3

子曰:“邦有道，危言危行；邦无道，危行言孙。”

15.11

颜渊问为邦。子曰:“行夏之时，乘殷之辂（**lù**），服周之冕，乐则《韶》《舞》。放郑声，远佞人。郑声淫，佞人殆。”

17.1

阳货欲见孔子，孔子不见，归（**kuì**）孔子豚。

孔子时其亡也，而往拜之，遇诸涂。谓孔子曰:“来！予与尔言。”

8.14 The Master said, "While not in office, do not discuss official policies."

13.5 The Master said, "A person may be able to recite three hundred verses from the *Book of Songs* by heart and yet fails when given administrative responsibilities and proves incapable of using his own initiative when sent as emissary to foreign states. If such is the case, then what use is it for him to recite so much of this book?"

13.17 On becoming the magistrate of Jufu, Zixia asked about government. The Master said, "Do not make haste. Do not covet small gains. Haste makes waste. Great tasks will not be accomplished if you covet small gains."

14.3 The Master said, "When the Way prevails in a state, act in an upright way and speak boldly. When the Way does not prevail, act in an upright way but speak with caution."

15.11 Yan Yuan asked how a state should be governed. The Master said, "Use the calendar of Xia, ride in the carriage of Yin, and wear the ceremonial cap of Zhou. As for music, play the *Shao* and *Wu*, abandon the tunes of *Zheng* and stay away from the flatterers. The tunes of *Zheng* are lascivious and the flatterers are dangerous."

17.1 Yang Huo wanted to see Confucius. When Confucius declined, Yang Huo sent him a steamed suckling pig.

Knowing that Yang was not at home, Confucius then went to his house to make a courtesy return call. On the way, the two happened to meet. Yang Huo said to Confucius, "Come now, I'll tell you something."

曰："怀其宝而迷其邦，可谓仁乎？"

曰："不可。""好从事而亟失时，可谓知乎？"

曰："不可。""日月逝矣，岁不我与。"

孔子曰："诺，吾将仕矣。"

Then he went on, "Can one be considered humane when he hides his talents and allows his country to go astray?" "I should say not," answered Confucius. "Can one be considered wise who is eager to be in government and yet misses his opportunity to do so time and again?" "I should say not," answered Confucius. Days and months rush by, and the years do not wait for us." added Yang Huo.

Confucius then said, "All right, I'll take up office."[1]

1 Yang Huo was a steward of the Jisun Family. For years, Yang Huo was in control of the State of Lu through his power over the Jisun Family. Yang Huo would like to invite Confucius to serve him, but Confucius, being reluctant, was trying to avoid meeting him.

九

君子与小人

IX

Man of honor (君子 *Junzi*) vs. the petty-minded man (小人 *Xiaoren*)

Confucius on the man of honor (君子*junzi*) and the petty-minded man (小人*xiaoren*)

These two terms used to be limited to describing people's social status, the former referring to members of the aristocracy and the latter referring to those of the underclass. In *The Analects*, Confucius gave these terms an ethical dimension. To Confucius, a man of honor is the ideal person who through his studies achieves self-improvement and becomes a beneficial member of the society. The petty-minded man is the former's antithesis. Hence, his behavior is harmful to the society. To illustrate his point, Confucius provides ample examples of their contrary manifestations in daily life.

In this respect, it is interesting to note that Confucius also used the terms good person (善人*shanren*) and sage (圣人 *shengren*) when referring to people whose quality is even superior to the man of honor.

16.8

孔子曰:“君子有三畏:畏天命,畏大人,畏圣人之言。小人不知天命而不畏也,狎大人,侮圣人之言。”

§9.1　何谓君子?君子标准

1.14

子曰:“君子食无求饱,居无求安,敏于事而慎于言,就有道而正焉,可谓好学也已。”

1.8

子曰:“君子,不重则不威;学则不固。主忠信,无友不如己者,过则勿惮改。”

Youhenzhe (有恒者) is also a positive term in *The Analects*.

In the present translation, when referring to people of the underclass, the term petty people are used to distinguish them from the petty-minded people.

16.8 Confucius said, "The man of honor holds three things in awe — the mandate of Heaven, people in high position and the words of sages. The petty-minded man, being ignorant of the mandate of Heaven, does not stand in awe of it. He treats people in high position with insolence and the words of the sages with disdain."

§ 9.1 What makes one a man of honor — criteria for being a *Junzi*.

1.14 The Master said, "The man of honor seeks neither a full belly nor a comfortable house. He is quick in action, but cautious with his words. He corrects his own mistakes by learning from those who know the Way. He can thus be regarded as studious."

1.8 The Master said, "A man of honor would not have commanded respect if he lacked seriousness, and even if he had studied hard, his learning would not have a firm foundation. He pays great attention to loyalty and faithfulness and does not accept as friends those who don't follow the same moral principles. When he makes a mistake, he is not afraid of correcting himself."

2.12

子曰:“君子不器。”

2.13

子贡问君子。子曰:“先行其言而后从之。”

3.7

子曰:“君子无所争,必也射乎!揖让而升,下而饮,其争也君子。”

4.24

子曰:“君子欲讷于言而敏于行。”

4.25

子曰:“德不孤,必有邻。”

5.16

子谓子产:“有君子之道四焉:其行己也恭,其事上也敬,其养民也惠,其使民也义。”

6.4

子华使于齐,冉子为其母请粟。子曰:“与之釜。”请益。曰:“与之庾。”冉子与之粟五秉。

2.12 The Master said, "A man of honor should not be a mere utensil[1]."

2.13 Zigong asked about the man of honor. The Master said, "He always puts his ideas into action before expressing them in words."

3.7 The Master said, "There is no contention between two men of honor. The only exception is perhaps archery. Even so, when the contest starts, the two archers bow to make way for each other. And when the contest ends, they drink and toast to each other. So they are quite like men of honor when they do contend."

4.24 The Master said, "The man of honor prefers to be slow in speech but quick in action."

4.25 The Master said, "The man of honor is never alone. He is sure to enjoy the company of friends."

5.16 When talking of Zi Chan[2], the Master said, "He had four virtues typical of a man of honor: he was humble in his manners, respectful to his sovereign, generous towards the common people and just in using their services."

6.4 Zi Hua[3] was sent on a mission to the State of Qi. Master Ran[4] asked for an allowance of millet for Zihua's mother. The Master said, "Give her some." The latter asked for more. The Master said, "Give her double the amount." Master Ran, however, gave her a hundred times more than required.

---

1 A utensil serves only to fulfil one specific purpose. According to Confucius, a man of honor should be more than a specialist. He should be able to handle different tasks and situations. Compare this concept with the Renaissance man in Europe.

2 A minister of the State of Zheng.

3 His background being linked in.

4 Ranjiu. Confuicus' disciple. His full name is Gongsun Chi.

子曰：“赤之适齐也，乘肥马，衣轻裘。吾闻之也：君子周急不继富。”

6.18

子曰：“质胜文则野，文胜质则史。文质彬彬，然后君子。”

6.26

宰我问曰：“仁者，虽告之曰：井有仁焉，其从之也？”

子曰：“何为其然也？君子可逝也，不可陷也；可欺也，不可罔也。”

6.27

子曰：“君子博学于文，约之以礼，亦可以弗畔矣夫。”

8.4

曾子有疾，孟敬子问之。曾子言曰：“鸟之将死，其鸣也哀；人之将死，其言也善。君子所贵乎道者三：动容貌，斯远暴慢矣；正颜色，斯近信矣；出辞气，斯远鄙倍矣。笾（biān）豆之事，则有司存。”

8.6

曾子曰：“可以托六尺之孤，可以寄百里之命，临大节而不可夺也。

The Master said, "Zi Hua is going to Qi in a grand style, in a carriage drawn by well-fed horses and dressed in fine furs. I have heard that a man of honor gives to help the needy, but not to make the rich richer."

6.18 The Master said, "Substance without refinement is uncouth. But refinement without substance is pedantic. Only when substance and refinement are well blended can there be a man of honor."

6.26 Zaiwo[1] asked, "If a man of honor were told that another of his kind had fallen into a well, would he jump in to save the latter?" The Master answered, "Why should that be? A man of honor will try to rescue the man in the well, but he won't jump in himself. He may be deceived, but he will not act foolishly."

6.27 The Master said, "The humane will not go astray, for he is widely read and cultured and he keeps himself in line with the rituals."

8.4 When Master Zeng was ill, Meng Jing Zi[2] visited him. Master Zeng said, "When a bird is about to die, its cries are mournful. When a man is about to die, his words are well-intended. There are three principles of conduct a man of honor values most. In appearance, be composed and thus avoid wantonness and tardiness; in demeanor, cling to good faith and thus invite trust; in speech, be careful with words and thus avoid vulgarity and impropriety. As to the details of liturgy, leave them to the minor officials who are in charge."

8.6 Master Zeng said, "If a person can be entrusted with an orphaned

---

1 Confucius' disciple.

2 A minister of Lu.

君子人与？君子人也。”

11.21

子曰：“论笃是与。君子者乎？色庄者乎？”

12.4

司马牛问君子。子曰：“君子不忧不惧。”

曰：“不忧不惧，斯谓之君子已乎？”

子曰：“内省不疚，夫何忧何惧？”

12.5

司马牛忧曰：“人皆有兄弟，我独亡。”

子夏曰：“商闻之矣：死生有命，富贵在天。君子敬而无失，与人恭而有礼，四海之内，皆兄弟也。君子何患乎无兄弟也？”

12.8

棘子成曰：“君子质而已矣，何以文为？”

子贡曰：“惜乎，夫子之说君子也，驷不及舌。文犹质也，质犹文也。

young ruler and the destiny of a state of a hundred square *li*[1], if he can be unyielding in moments of crisis, then he is indeed a man of honor."

11.21 The Master said, "I applaud someone who speaks sincerely. However, is he truly a man of honor, or is he simply putting on a dignified look?"

12.4 Sima Niu[2] asked about being a man of honor. The Master said, "A man of honor is free from worries and fears."

Sima Niu asked, "Can one be called a man of honor simply because he is free from worries and fears?"

The Master said, "If one has a clear conscience, what has he to worry about and fear?"

12.5 Sima Niu complained, "Others have brothers, I alone have none." Zixia said to him, "I have heard it said that life and death are decided by fate; wealth and rank decreed by Heaven. The man of honor is dedicated to his work, does nothing wrong and is respectful and polite to others. Thus, all people within the Four Seas are his brothers. Why, then, does he have to worry about not having any brothers?"

12.8 Ji Zicheng[3] said, "The important thing about a man of honor is his good intrinsic quality. (When he has this quality), what need is there for cultural refinement?"

Zigong said, "What a pity that you should talk about a man of honor in such a way. A word once spoken cannot be overtaken even by a team of four horses. (To a man of honor), cultural

1 One *li* equals 0.5 kilometer, or 0.311 mile.

2 Confucius's disciple.

3 Minister of Wei.

虎豹之鞟（kuò）犹犬羊之鞟。”

12.24

曾子曰:“君子以文会友，以友辅仁。”

14.5

南宫适（kuò）问于孔子曰:“羿善射，奡（ào）荡舟，俱不得其死然。禹稷躬稼而有天下。”夫子不答。

南宫适出。子曰:“君子哉若人！尚德哉若人！”

14.26

子曰:“不在其位，不谋其政。”

曾子曰:“君子思不出其位。”

14.27

子曰:“君子耻其言而过其行。”

14.42

子路问君子。子曰:“修己以敬。”

曰:“如斯而已乎？”曰:“修己以安人。”

曰:“如斯而已乎？”曰:“修己以安百姓。修己以安百姓，尧舜其犹病诸？”

refinement is just as important as his intrinsic quality. The skin of a tiger or leopard would be no difference from that of a dog or sheep once its colorful fur is shorn."[1]

12.24 Master Zeng said, "A man of honor makes friends through his learning and looks to friends for support in cultivating humaneness."

14.5 Nangong Kuo asked Confucius, "Yi was an excellent archer. Ao was skilled in sailing. Both met an untimely death. Yu and Ji, on the other hand, farmed the land. Both won the empire. (What conclusion can one draw from this?)" The Master gave no answer.

After Nangong Kuo had left, the Master said, "What a man of honor he is! How he upholds virtue!"

14.26 Confucius said, "While not in office, do not discuss official policies." Zeng Zi commented, "The man of honor would never contemplate overstepping his position."

14.27 The Master said, "The man of honor considers it a disgrace to let his words outstrip his deeds."

14.42 Zilu asked about the man of honor. The Master said, "The man of honor cultivates himself to become respectable."

Zilu asked, "Is that all?"

"He cultivates himself and thereby brings peace and security to his fellow men."

"Is that all?"

"He cultivates himself and thereby brings peace and security to the common people. And to do this is hard to accomplish even

1 Fur is used here as a metaphor for cultural refinement.

15.18

子曰:“君子义以为质，礼以行之，孙以出之，信以成之。君子哉！”

15.19

子曰:“君子病无能焉，不病人之不己知也。”

15.20

子曰:“君子疾没世而名不称焉。”

15.22

子曰:“君子矜而不争，群而不党。”

15.23

子曰:“君子不以言举人，不以人废言。”

15.32

子曰:“君子谋道不谋食。耕也，馁在其中矣；学也，禄在其中矣。君子忧道不忧贫。”

15.37

子曰:“君子贞而不谅。”

16.7

孔子曰:“君子有三戒：少之时，血气未定，戒之在色；及其壮也，血气方刚，戒之在斗；及其老也，血气既衰，戒之在得。”

for the sage kings, Yao and Shun."

15.18 The Master said, "The man of honor takes righteousness as his basic principle. He practises it by observing the rituals, gives it expression by being modest and brings it to fruition by being trustworthy. That, indeed, is what a man of honor does."

15.19 The Master said, "A man of honor fears his own insufficiencies, not the failure of others to understand him."

15.20 The Master said, "A man of honor worries that he might depart from this world without leaving a name."

15.22 The Master said, "A man of honor is dignified but not contentious; he is sociable but not clannish."

15.23 The Master said, "A man of honor does not approve of a person because he expresses an opinion to his liking, nor does he reject an opinion because it is held by a person he dislikes."

15.32 The Master said, "The man of honor seeks the Way. He is not concerned with making a living. Farm the land and you end up being hungry. Study and you end up being an official with earnings. The man of honor is worried about not finding the Way, rather than about living in poverty."

15.37 The Master said, "The man of honor is principled but he is not rigid about small matters."

16.7 Confucius said, "The man of honor must guard against three dangers. When young, while the vital spirits are not yet settled, he should guard against lust. In the prime of life, during which the vital spirits are exuberant, he should guard against contentiousness. In old age, when the vital spirits are in decline, he should guard against greed."

16.10

孔子曰:“君子有九思:视思明,听思聪,色思温,貌思恭,言思忠,事思敬,疑思问,忿思难,见得思义。”

17.24

子贡曰:“君子亦有恶(wù)乎?”子曰:“有恶。恶称人之恶者,恶居下流而讪(shàn)上者,恶勇而无礼者,恶果敢而窒者。”

曰:“赐也亦有恶乎?”“恶徼以为知者,恶不孙以为勇者,恶讦(jié)以为直者。”

§9.2 何谓小人?

17.12

子曰:“色厉而内荏,譬诸小人,其犹穿窬(yú)之盗也与?”

17.15

子曰:“鄙夫可与事君也与哉?其未得之也,患得之。既得之,患失

16.10 Confucius said, "There are nine occasions which call for careful consideration by the man of honor: When using his eyes, is he seeing clearly? When using his ears, is he hearing distinctly? Regarding his countenance, does he look amiable? In his demeanor, does he appear reverent? When he speaks to people, is he sincere? In performing his duties, is he conscientious? When in doubt, does he seek answers from others? When in rage, does he consider its possible consequences. When faced with gain, does he ask himself whether it is his due."

17.24 Zigong asked, "Is there anything that the man of honor detests?" The Master answered, "Yes, there is. He detests those who go about publicizing the misdeeds of others. He detests those inferiors who slander their superiors. He detests those who possess courage but lack the spirit of the rituals. He detests those who are resolute but stubborn."

The Master then asked, "Zigong, is there anything you detest?" Zigong answered, "I detest those who consider themselves wise in plagiarising other people's works, courageous in being rude, and forthright in exposing others' privacy."

§ 9.2 Traits of the petty-minded man.

17.12 The Master said, "A coward who puts on a brave face is a petty man. Isn't he like the thief who breaks in by digging a hole in the wall?"

17.15 The Master said, "How can one collaborate with a rogue while

之。苟患失之，无所不至矣。”

17.25

子曰：“唯女子与小人为难养也，近之则不孙，远之则怨。”

§9.3 君子较之小人

2.14

子曰：“君子周而不比，小人比而不周。”

4.11

子曰：“君子怀德，小人怀土；君子怀刑，小人怀惠。”

4.16

子曰：“君子喻于义，小人喻于利。”

6.13

子谓子夏曰：“女为君子儒，无为小人儒。”

serving the sovereign? Before the rogue gets what he wants, he worries that he might not get it. After he has got it, he worries that he might lose it. Thus, in order to preserve it, he would be ready to go to extremes."

17.25 The Master said, "Women and the petty men are especially difficult to deal with. They become insolent if you get too close to them, but if you keep them at a distance, they complain."

§ 9.3 Difference between a man of honor and a petty-minded person.

2.14 The Master said, "A man of honor associates with many but does not form a clique; the petty-minded man does the opposite."

4.11 The Master said, "The man of honor cherishes virtue, the petty man cherishes his land. The man of honor is concerned about the sanctions of law, the petty-minded man about the favors he hopes to receive."

4.16 The Master said, "The man of honor thinks in terms of righteousness. The petty-minded man in terms of gains."

6.13 The Master said, "Be an honorable scholar, not a petty-minded pedant."

7.37

子曰:“君子坦荡荡，小人长戚戚。”

12.16

子曰:“君子成人之美，不成人之恶。小人反是。”

13.23

子曰:“君子和而不同，小人同而不和。”

13.25

子曰:“君子易事而难说也。说之不以道，不说也；及其使人也，器之。小人难事而易说也。说之虽不以道，说也；及其使人也，求备焉。”

13.26

子曰:“君子泰而不骄，小人骄而不泰。”

14.6

子曰:“君子而不仁者有矣夫，未有小人而仁者也。”

14.23

子曰:“君子上达，小人下达。”

15.2

在陈绝粮，从者病，莫能兴。子路愠（yùn）见曰:“君子亦有穷乎？”子曰:“君子固穷，小人穷斯滥矣。”

7.37 The Master said, "The man of honor has peace of mind, while the petty-minded man is constantly troubled by anxiety."

12.16 The Master said, "A man of honor helps others to realize their best aims, but not their worst desires. A petty-minded man does the opposite."

13.23 The Master said, "A man of honor seeks harmony but not identity of views; a petty-minded man seeks identity but not true harmony."

13.25 The Master said, "A man of honor is easy to serve but hard to please. If one tries to please him by means which are not in accord with the Way, he will not be pleased. When it comes to selecting someone for a job, he will base his choice on the person's capability and virtue. The petty-minded man is difficult to serve but easy to please. He will be pleased even if one goes against the Way. But when it comes to using such people, he is forever picking faults."

13.26 The Master said, "A man of honor is composed but not arrogant. A petty-minded man is arrogant but not composed."

14.6 The Master said, "We have seen cases of a man of honor not being humane occasionally, but we have never seen a petty-minded man being humane."

14.23 The Master said, "The man of honor reaches for higher things. The petty-minded man reaches for lower things."

15.2 While in the state of Chen, Confucius ran out of provisions. His disciples were so weakened that they could not stand on their feet. Zilu came to see Confucius and complained, "Does the man of honor have to suffer from hunger, too?" The Master answered,

15.21

子曰:“君子求诸己，小人求诸人。”

15.34

子曰:“君子不可小知而可大受也，小人不可大受而可小知也。”

17.23

子路曰:“君子尚勇乎?”子曰:“君子义以为上。君子有勇而无义为乱，小人有勇而无义为盗。”

"When the man of honor bears hunger, he is undisturbed. But the petty-minded man throws caution to the wind whenever in want."

15.21 The Master said, "A man of honor sets demands on himself while a petty-minded man sets demands on others."

15.34 The Master said, "The man of honor can be entrusted with great responsibilities but sometimes fails in small matters. The petty-minded man can be entrusted with small matters but often fails in great responsibilities."

17.23 Zilu asked, "Does The man of honor value courage?" The Master said, "The man of honor considers justice the supreme good. Courage without justice would cause high-ranking people to resort to revolt. It would turn the petty men to banditry."

十

士之责

10.1 士

2.18

子张学干禄，子曰："多闻阙疑，慎言其余，则寡尤；多见阙殆，慎行其余，则寡悔。言寡尤，行寡悔，禄在其中矣。"

2.21

或谓孔子曰："子奚不为政？"

子曰："《书》云：'孝乎惟孝，友于兄弟，施于有政，是亦为政。"

X

Role and Duty of the Scholar/Official (士 *shi*)

10.1 Scholar / Official (士 *shi*).

In ancient China, *Shi* refered to those in the social stratum between the aristocracy / high-ranking officials and the common people. They became scholars and later served in the government either as officials or warriors.

2.18 Zizhang[1] asked the Master how to be an official. The Master replied, "Listen to all kinds of opinions, set aside what is dubious and speak discreetly on the rest. That way, you will make few mistakes. Open your eyes wide, set aside what is dubious and act on the rest with caution. You will then have few regrets. Since a good official makes few mistakes, his success is ensured."

2.21 Asked why he had not become involved in government, the Master answered, "The *Book of Historical Documents* says, 'Piety

1 Confucius' disciple.

奚其为为政？”

4.9

子曰：“士志于道，而耻恶衣恶食者，未足与议也。”

8.7

曾子曰：“士不可以不弘毅，任重而道远。仁以为己任，不亦重乎？死而后已，不亦远乎？”

8.12

子曰：“三年学，不至于谷，不易得也。”

12.20

子张问：“士何如斯可谓之达矣？”

子曰：“何哉，尔所谓达者？”

子张对曰：“在邦必闻，在家必闻。”

子曰：“是闻也，非达也。夫达也者，质直而好义，察言而观色，虑以下人。在邦必达，在家必达。夫闻也者，色取仁而行违，居之不疑。在邦必闻，在家必闻。”

13.20

子贡问曰：“何如斯可谓之士矣？”

means being filial to your parents and being fraternal to your brothers; spreading this idea will exert an influence upon the government.' If that is so, why must I take part in government?"

4.9 The Master said, "There is no point in soliciting the opinion of a scholar whose mind is set on learning the Way and yet is ashamed of his having to eat coarse grain and wear shabby clothes."

8.7 Master Zeng said, "A scholar must be strong and steadfast, for his burden is heavy and his journey long. Since his task is to practise humaneness, is the burden not heavy? Since till death does his journey end, is it not long?"

8.12 The Master said, "It is hard to find one who has studied for three years without thinking about his career."

12.20 Zizhang asked, "What must a scholar do to become prestigious?"

The Master asked him, "What is your understanding of prestigious?"

Zizhang answered, "To be well-known whether serving the state or the big family."

"But that is only being well-known and not prestigious. To win prestige, one must be upright and just, sensitive to others'words and observant of their moods and expressions, and always ready to give precedence to others. Such a person is sure to win prestige whether he serves the state or a noble family. A well-known person may put on an appearance of being honorable, but acts to the contrary, and feels no qualms about it. Such a person can make himself well-known, in or out of government."

13.20 Zigong asked, "What kind of a person deserves to be called a scholar?"

子曰："行已有耻，使于四方，不辱君命，可谓士矣。"
曰："敢问其次。"
曰："宗族称孝焉，乡党称弟焉。"
曰"敢问其次。"
曰："言必信，行必果，硁硁（kēng）然小人哉！抑亦可以为次矣。"
曰："今之从政者何如？"子曰："噫！斗筲（shāo）之人，何足算也？"

13.28

子路问曰："何如斯可谓之士矣？"
子曰："切切偲偲（sī），怡怡如也，可谓士矣。朋友切切偲偲，兄弟怡怡。"

14.2

子曰："士而怀居，不足以为士矣。"

14.22

子路问事君。子曰："勿欺也，而犯之。"

14.38

子路宿于石门。晨门曰："奚自？"
子路曰："自孔氏。"
曰："是知其不可而为之者与？"

The Master said, "A person who has a sense of shame and, when sent abroad by his sovereign, accomplishes his mission, can be called a scholar."

"May I ask, what about the next down the scale?"

"Someone who is praised by his clan as a good son and, in his village, as being respectful to his elders."

"What about the next?"

"Someone who keeps his word and acts resolutely so that whatever he undertakes, he brings it to fruition, may make up the next even if he is stubbornly petty-minded."

"What about those in government today?"

"Oh, they are so narrow-minded and of such limited capacity that they hardly count."

13.28 Zilu asked, "What kind of a person can be called a scholar?"

The Master answered, "One who is exacting yet cordial toward others can be called a scholar. He is exacting toward his friends and cordial toward his brothers."

14.2 The Master said, "He who seeks material comfort is not qualified to be a scholar."

14.22 Zilu asked about the way to serve a sovereign. The Master said, "Do not deceive him (by feigning compliance). Rather, tell him the truth even if it offends him."

14.38 Zilu stayed for the night at the Stone Gate. The next morning, the gatekeeper asked him, "Where are you from?"

Zilu answered, "From Confucius."

The gatekeeper asked, "Is he the man who persists, knowing that his cause is hopeless?"

15.38

子曰:“事君，敬其事而后其食。”

19.1

子张曰:“士见危致命，见得思义，祭思敬，丧思哀，其可已矣。”

19.13

子夏曰:“仕而优则学，学而优则仕。”

20.2

子张问孔子曰:“何如斯可以从政矣?”

子曰:“尊五美，屏四恶，斯可以从政矣。”

子张曰:“何谓五美?”

子曰:“君子惠而不费，劳而不怨，欲而不贪，泰而不骄，威而不猛。”

子张曰:“何谓惠而不费?”

子曰:“因民之所利而利之，斯不亦惠而不费乎?择可劳而劳之，又

15.38 The Master said, “When serving the sovereign, attach great importance to the performance of your duties. How much you get for remuneration is secondary.”

19.1 Zizhang said, “What more could be asked of a scholar who is ready to lay down his life in the face of danger, who keeps righteousness in mind when there’s opportunity for gain, and who shows reverence while performing sacrificial ceremonies and who shows sorrow at mourning.”

19.13 Zixia said, “A good scholar should make a good official, a good official should continue with his studies.”

20.2 Zizhang asked Confucius, “How does one qualify for a government official?”

The Master said, “The qualifications are: Respect the five virtues and spurn the four evils.”

“What do you mean by the five virtues?” asked Zizhang.

The Master answered, “The man of honor is generous without excesses. He makes people work without causing them to complain. He is ambitious without being greedy. He is self-possessed without being arrogant. He is awe-inspiring without being fierce.”

“What do you mean by being generous without excesses?” asked Zizhang.

The Master answered, “If you let the common people do what is beneficial for them, isn’t it being generous without excesses? If you make people work on tasks they are capable of accomplishing, who will complain? If your ambition is to attain humaneness, there would be no place for greediness. The man of honor puts the many on a par with the few, the high on a par

谁怨？欲仁而得仁，又焉贪？君子无众寡，无大小，无敢慢，斯不亦泰而不骄乎？君子正其衣冠，尊其瞻视，俨然人望而畏之，斯不亦威而不猛乎？”

子张曰：“何谓四恶？”

子曰：“不教而杀，谓之虐；不戒视成，谓之暴；慢令致期，谓之贼；犹之与人也，出纳之吝，谓之有司。”

§10.2 儒、隐士、善人

with the low and dares not to be negligent, isn't that being self-possessed without being arrogant? The man of honor dresses properly and looks dignified, his solemnity causing fear. Isn't he awe-inspiring without being fierce?"

Zizhang asked"What do you mean by the four evils then?"

The Master answered, "To impose the death penalty without first educating the people amounts to cruelty. To demand achievement without prior requirements amounts to tyranny. To suddenly impose a deadline on a job without previous warning amounts to theft. To act miserly when it comes to giving amounts to stinginess."

§ 10.2 Ru (儒) / Hermit (隐士) / Good person (善人).

Confucius On Ru (儒), Hermit (隐士) and Good person (善人)

Ru used to refer to persons who officiated at rituals and funerals and even performed weather forecasting. Later, it became a term for scholars who taught the six arts to the children of officials. Still later, and after Confucius' death, there developed the school of Confucian thought known in Chinese as Ruism (儒家*rujia*) and translated into English as Confucianism.

Hermits were people and scholars and even members of the aristocracy who became disaffected with the state of affairs in the country or who wished to abstain from power in the royal court. They therefore withdrew themselves from the center of social activities and led a

6.13

子谓子夏曰:“女为君子儒，无为小人儒。”

7.26

子曰:“圣人吾不得而见之矣；得见君子者，斯可矣。”

子曰:“善人吾不得而见之矣；得见有恒者，斯可矣。亡而为有，虚而为盈，约而为泰，难乎有恒矣。”

11.20

子张问善人之道，子曰:“不践迹，亦不入于室。”

13.29

子曰:“善人教民七年，亦可以即戎矣。”

13.30

子曰:“以不教民战，是谓弃之。”

carefree life in faraway places.

In *The Analects*, they often criticized Confucius. The latter, while understanding their views, objected to this negative attitude toward political life. He once said to his disciple Zilu that there was no getting away from society since "We cannot keep company only with birds and beasts."

The good man (善人*shanren*) is a positive term for Confucius. In Confucius' ideology, the good man is, in some aspects, even harder to achieve than the man of honor.

6.13 The Master said, "Be an honorable scholar, not a petty-minded pedant."

7.26 The Master said, "I cannot hope to meet a sage. Meeting a man of honor would give me satisfaction."
He added, "I cannot hope to meet a good man. Meeting a man who sticks to his principles would give me satisfaction. A man can hardly stick to his principles if he pretends to be full when he's empty and to be at ease when he is in difficult circumstance."

11.20 Zizhang asked Confucius to define a good man. The Master answered, "He does not tread in the footsteps of others, nor does he gain entrance into the inner chamber."[1]

13.29 The Master said, "After being trained by a good man for seven years, the common people should be able to fight any battle."

13.30 The Master said, "To send people to war without giving them proper training is like throwing their lives away."

---

1 Implying that without applying himself to study, even a man of good nature cannot know the Way.

14.37

子曰:“贤者辟世,其次辟地,其次辟色,其次辟言。”

子曰:“作者七人矣。”

18.5

楚狂接舆歌而过孔子曰:“凤兮凤兮,何德之衰!往者不可谏,来者犹可追。已而已而!今之从政者殆而!”

孔子下,欲与之言。趋而辟之,不得与之言。

18.6

长沮、桀溺耦而耕。孔子过之,使子路问津焉。

长沮曰:“夫执舆者为谁?”

子路曰:“为孔丘。”

曰:“是鲁孔丘与?”

曰:“是也。”

曰:“是知津矣。”

问于桀溺。

14.37 The Master said, "To some wise men (meaning the hermits), the highest form of wisdom is to shun the society. Next, to shun certain places. Next, to shun certain looks. And finally, to shun certain words. Seven men have accomplished this feat."

18.5 Jie Yu, "the Madman of Chu," passed by Confucius' carriage, singing:
"Oh phoenix, my phoenix!
How your virtue has waned!
The past is beyond retrieve,
The future has yet to come.
Worry not, worry not.
There is nothing but danger
For those in power today."
Confucius stepped down, intending to speak to the "madman". But the man hurried off and Confucius never got to speak to him.[1]

18.6 Chang Ju and Jie Ni were ploughing the land together, yoked as a team. Walking past them, Confucius sent Zilu to ask them where the ford was.
Chang Ju asked, "Who is that driving the carriage?"
Zilu said, "It is Confucius."
"Then he must be the Confucius of Lu."
"He is."
"Then he should know where the ford is."[2]
Zilu then turned to Jie Ni.

1 Jie Yu was a hermit. In ancient times, it was believed that the phoenix would appear when the Way prevailed in the world. Jie Yu was comparing Confucius to a phoenix that refused to disappear even though the Way no longer prevailed. That's why he considered Confucius' virtue had waned.

2 Implying that since Confucius is much traveled, he should be familiar with the place's terrain.

桀溺曰："子为谁？"

曰："为仲由。"

曰："是孔丘之徒与？"

对曰："然。"

曰："滔滔者天下皆是也，而谁以易之？且而与其从辟人之士也，岂若从辟世之士哉？"耰（yōu）而不辍。

子路行以告。

夫子怃然曰："鸟兽不可与同群，吾非斯人之徒与而谁与？天下有道，丘不与易也。"

Jie Ni asked, “Who are you?”

“I’m Zilu.”

“Then you must be a student of Confucius of Lu?”

Zilu answered, “I am.”

“The world is now as turbulent as a river in spate. Who is there to change it? Rather than following a person who is trying to get away from one bad sovereign to another, wouldn’t it be better for you to follow someone who tries to get away from the bad world?” So saying, Jie Ni continued with his harrowing.

Zilu went back to report what he had heard to Confucius.

The Master was lost in thought. Afterwards, he said, “We cannot keep company only with birds and beasts. Who else should we have for company but people? Once the Way prevails in the world, you and I will have no need to try and change it.”

十一

孔子的评论

XI

Confucius' Comments

§ 11.1　评古今之时

6.24

子曰:“齐一变，至于鲁；鲁一变，至于道。”

7.15

冉有曰:“夫子为卫君乎?”子贡曰:“诺，吾将问之。”入，曰:“伯夷、叔齐何人也?”

曰:“古之贤人也。”

曰:“怨乎?”

曰:“求仁而得仁，又何怨。”

出，曰:“夫子不为也。”

8.16

子曰:“狂而不直，侗（tóng）而不愿，悾悾而不信，吾不知之矣。

14.19

子言卫灵公之无道也，康子曰:“夫如是，奚而不丧?”

孔子曰:“仲叔圉（yǔ）治宾客，祝鮀治宗庙，王孙贾治军旅。夫如是，奚其丧?”

§ 11.1 About the time he lived in and before.

6.24 The Master said, "With reform, the State of Qi can equal Lu; with reform, Lu can attain the Way."[1]

7.15 Ranyou wanted to know if the Master supported the Lord of Wei. Zigong said, "Alright, I shall go and find out."

He went in and asked, "What sort of people were Bo Yi and Shu Qi?"

The Master answered, "Men of virtue in ancient times."

Zigong asked, "Did they have any regret?"

"They sought to be humane and they attained their goal. Why should they have any regret?"

On coming out, Zigong said, "The Master does not support the Lord of Wei."[2]

8.16 The Master said, "Men who are ambitious but are not upright, men who are ignorant yet inattentive, men who are incapable and untrustworthy—these are people I cannot appreciate."

14.19 The Master was speaking about the unprincipled course of Duke Ling of Wei when Ji Kangzi asked, "If that's the case, why did he not lose his state?"

Confucius answered, "He had Zhong Shuyu in charge of foreign affairs, Zhu Tao of ancestral sacrifice and Gongsun Jia of military

---

1 Lu, whose first duke being the son of Duke Zhou, was considered by Confucius as the model of Duke Zhou's tradition.

2 Confucius did not support the Lord of Wei because he fought against his own father for the throne, whereas the brothers Bo Yi and Shu Qi both declined to ascend the throne.

17.16

子曰:“古者民有三疾，今也或是之亡也。古之狂也肆，今之狂也荡；古之矜也廉，今之矜也忿戾；古之愚也直，今之愚也诈而已矣。”

§11.2 评古今之人

affairs. That being the case, how could he lose his state?"

17.16 The Master said, "In ancient times, the common people had three faults, but even these faults have worsened today. The arrogant were reckless, but now they have become dissolute. The conceited were unpromising, but now they have become perverse. The foolish were straight, but now they have become deceptive."

§ 11.2 About historical and contemporary figures.

Confucius on historical and contemporary figures

In *The Analects*, Confucius made numerous comments on historical as well as contemporary figures when referring to them to his disciples. Through these observations, he noted their merits and demerits and thus conveyed his own political thesis in a round-about way.

For example, Guan Zhong of the State of Qi was a noted statesman who had significant impact on the political situation during the Spring and Autumn Period. So was Zicang of the State of Zheng. Confucius discussed their pluses and minuses in great detail and, in so doing, demonstrated what he meant by humane government. As to the Duke of Zhou, who assisted his nephew King Cheng in the early formative stage of the Zhou Dynasty, he was Confucius' role model. Confucius once lamented that he was getting old because he no longer dreamt about the Duke of Zhou. So were the earliest rulers Yao, Shun and Yu whom he praised in lavish terms.

3.22

子曰:“管仲之器小哉!”

或曰:“管仲俭乎?”

曰:“管氏有三归,官事不摄,焉得俭?”

“然则管仲知礼乎?”

曰:“邦君树塞门,管氏亦树塞门;邦君为两君之好有反坫,管氏亦有反坫。管氏而知礼,孰不知礼?”

5.23

子曰:“伯夷叔齐不念旧恶,怨是用希。”

5.24

子曰:“孰谓微生高直?或乞醯(xī)焉,乞诸其邻而与之。”

5.26

颜渊、季路侍。子曰:“盍各言尔志。”

子路曰:“愿车马衣轻裘与朋友共,敝之而无憾。”

The full range of his comments on numerous figures and events showed that Confucius was not only very knowledgeable about China's ancient history, he also kept himself abreast of the panorama of political events of his own time.

3.22 The Master said, "Guan Zhong[1] had little capacity.

Someone asked, "Wasn't Guan Zhong frugal?"

The Master answered, "Guan Zhong had a large income from rents and a multitude of attendants. How could he be said to be frugal?"

"Didn't he know the rituals well?"

The Master answered, "The ruler of a state had screens; so did Guan Zhong. The former ruler had stands for emptied wine cups when he entertained other rulers; so did Guan Zhong. If you think Guan Zhong knew the rituals, then who doesn't?"

5.23 The Master said, "The brothers Bo Yi and Shu Qi bore no grudges against others for their past wrongs and that's why they incurred little ill will."

5.24 The Master said, "Who said Weisheng Gao[2] was straight forward? Once when someone wanted to borrow some vinegar from him, instead of saying that he didn't have any, he borrowed some from his neighbor and gave it to that man."

5.26 Yan Hui and Zilu were with Confucius when he said, "Now tell me what you wish for most."

Zilu said, "I wish to share with my friends my carriages and horses, my clothes and furs, and never complain even if they spoil them."

---

1 Chief minister of the State of Qi.

2 Somebody in the State of Lu.

颜渊曰:“愿无伐善，无施劳。”
子路曰:“愿闻子之志。”
子曰:“老者安之，朋友信之，少者怀之。”

6.15

子曰:“孟之反不伐，奔而殿，将入门，策其马，曰：非敢后也，马不进也。”

6.16

子曰:“不有祝鮀（tuó）之佞，而有宋朝之美，难乎免于今之世矣。”

8.21

子曰:“禹，吾无间然矣。菲饮食而致孝乎鬼神，恶衣服而致美乎黼(fǔ）冕，卑宫室而尽力沟洫（xù)。禹，吾无间然矣”

5.17

子曰:“晏平仲善与人交，久而敬之。”

13.8

子谓卫公子荆:“善居室。始有，曰:‘苟合矣’。少有，曰:‘苟完矣。’

Yan Hui said, "I wish never to boast of my merits or show off what I have done."

Zilu asked the Master, "What is your fondest wish?"

Confucius said, "I wish for the old to live in peace and comfort, for friends to trust each other, and for the young to be taken care of."

6.15 The Master said, "Meng Zhifan[1] was never given to boasting about himself. Once, when his army was retreating, he stayed in the rear to cover his forces. But as they approached their own city gate, he goaded his horse on, shouting, 'I stayed at the rear not out of courage, it is just that my horse wouldn't go any faster.'"

6.16 The Master said, "In today's world, it would be difficult for you to escape trouble if you had only the good looks of Song Chao[2] but not the eloquence of Zhu Tuo[3]."

8.21 The Master said, "With Yu I can find no fault. He ate simple food but offered grand sacrifices to the ancestral spirit. He wrote coarse clothes but dressed magnificently on sacrificial occasions. He lived in a humble house but devoted his all to fighting the floods. With Yu I can find no fault."

5.17 The Master said, "Yan Pingzhong[4] was good at making friends. The longer the friendship, the more he respected his friends."

13.8 Speaking of Prince Jing of Wei, the Master said, "He knew how

1 A minister of Lu.

2 A prince of the State of Song who had twice caused great disturbance in his country because of his good looks and illicit affairs with Nanzi.

3 A minister of Wei.

4 A minister of Qi.

富有，曰：‘苟美矣。’”

14.8

子曰：“为命，裨谌（bì chén）草创之，世叔讨论之，行人子羽修饰之，东里子产润色之。”

14.11

子曰：“孟公绰为赵、魏老则优，不可以为滕、薛大夫。”

14.14

子曰：“臧武仲以防求为后于鲁，虽曰不要君，吾不信也。”

14.18

公叔文子之臣大夫僎（xún），与文子同升诸公。子闻之，曰：“可以为‘文’矣。”

14.25

蘧（qú）伯玉使人于孔子，孔子与之坐而问焉。曰：“夫子何为？”
对曰：“夫子欲寡其过而未能也。”
使者出，子曰：“使乎！使乎！”

to manage his property. When he began to have some means, he said, 'It is enough.' When he had a little more, he said, 'It is quite adequate.' When he became prosperous, he said, 'It is excellent!'"[1]

14.8 The Master said, "When it came to issuing an edict (in the state of Zheng), Pi Chen wrote the first draft, Shi Shu discussed the content and put forward suggestions, Zi Yu, master of protocol, revised it and Zi Chan polished it."[2]

14.11 The Master said, "Meng Gongchuo[3] would be more than adequate serving as a steward of the Zhao or Wei family. But he would not be adequate serving as a minister even in small states like Teng or Xue."

14.14 The Master said, "Zang Wuzhong made his fief Fang coerce the Duke of Lu to agree to appoint the successor to Zang's family line a minister. Someone said this was not coercion. I disagree."

14.18 Zhuan, the steward of Gongshu Wenzi, was promoted to a ministerial post (of Wei) along with his master. On hearing this, the Master said, "Now, Wenzi deserves the title'Wen' (of being cultured)."

14.25 Qu Boyu[4] sent a messenger to Confucius. After giving him a seat, Confucius asked, "How is your master?" The messenger answered, "My master tries to make fewer mistakes but has not yet succeeded."

---

1 Prince Jing was a senior official of Wei. Among the ministers, embezzlement and extravagance were common. Therefore, Confucius praised Prince Jing's simple and frugal life style.

2 All three were officials of Zheng.

3 A senior minister of Lu.

4 A minister of Wei.

15.7

子曰:“直哉史鱼!邦有道如矢,邦无道如矢,君子哉蘧伯玉!邦有道则仕;邦无道则可卷而怀之。”

18.2

柳下惠为士师,三黜。人曰:“子未可以去乎?”曰:“直道而事人,焉往而不三黜?枉道而事人,何必去父母之邦?”

18.10

周公谓鲁公曰:“君子不施其亲,不使大臣怨乎不以。故旧无大故,则不弃也。无求备于一人。”

18.11

周有八士:伯达、伯适、伯突、仲忽、叔夜、叔夏、季随、季娲。

5.15

子贡问曰:“孔文子何以谓之文也?”

子曰:“敏而好学,不耻下问,是以谓之文也。”

After he left, the Master said repeatedly, "What an excellent messenger!"

15.7 The Master said, "How straight Shi Yu[1] was! When the Way prevailed, he was as straight as an arrow. When the Way did not prevail, he remained the same. And what a man of honor Qu Boyu was! When the Way prevailed, he took office. When the Way did not prevail, he folded up and lived in seclusion."

18.2 Liuxia Hui was a judge who had been removed from office time and again. Someone said to him, "Why don't you go somewhere else?" He answered, "If, in the course of my service elsewhere, I refuse to change my way, would I be able to avoid the same fate? If I agreed to change my way, then there would be no need to leave the land of my parents."

18.10 The Duke of Zhou told (his son) the Duke of Lu, "The sovereign does not neglect his relatives, nor would he let his ministers complain of not having his trust. Unless they make serious mistakes, those who have served for long years should not be dismissed. Do not demand perfection from any individual."

18.11 There were eight great scholars during the Zhou Dynasty: Bo Da, Bo Kuo, Zhong Tu, Zhong Hu, Shu Ye, Shu Xia, Ji Sui and Ji Gua.

5.15 Zigong asked, "Why was Kong Wenzi[2] called Wenzi[3]?"
The Master answered, "Because he was smart, eager to learn and was never ashamed to learn from those below his rank. That's why he was honored as Wenzi."

---

1 A minster of the State of Wei.

2 A minister of the State of Wei.

3 A minister of Wei, posthumously named as Weizi, the cultured one.

5.16

子谓子产:“有君子之道四焉:其行己也恭,其事上也敬,其养民也惠,其使民也义。”

5.18

子曰:“臧文仲居蔡,山节藻梲(zhuō),何如其知也!”

5.19

子张问曰:“令尹子文三仕为令尹,无喜色;三已之,无愠色。旧令尹之政,必以告新令尹。何如?”

子曰:“忠矣。”

曰:“仁矣乎?”

曰:“未知。焉得仁?”

“崔子弑齐君,陈子文有马十乘,弃而违之,至于他邦,则曰:‘犹吾大夫崔子也。’违之。之一邦,则又曰:‘犹吾大夫崔子也。’违之,

5.16 When talking of Zi Chan[1], the Master said, "He had four virtues typical of a man of honor: he was humble in his manners, respectful to his sovereign, generous towards the common people and just in using their services."

5.18 The Master said, "Zang Wenzhong[2] kept a large tortoise in his house and for this pet, he had hills painted on the pillars and duckweeds on the raft posts. What is one to think of his intelligence?"[3]

5.19 Zizhang asked, "Zi Wen[4] gave no sign of pleasure on the three occa-sions when he was appointed Chief Minister, nor did he look unhappy on the three occasions when he was dismissed from that office. Moreover, before leaving his post, he always told his successors what had been done during his term of office. What do you think of him?"

The Master answered, "We can say that he was loyal."

Zizhang asked, "Can we say he was humane?"

The Master answered, "I don't know whether that can be called humaneness."

Zizhang asked again, "When Cui Zi[5] assassinated Duke Zhuang (of Qi), Chen Wenzi[6] abandoned his ten carriages and left. After he arrived in another state, he said, 'The officials here are no better than Minister Cui Zi.' He left and went to yet another

---

1 A minister of the State of Zheng.

2 A minister of Lu.

3 The ancients in China worshipped the tortoise for its longevity, the bigger they were, the more precious. Here, Confucius was critical of Zang Wenzhong for, according to the rituals, only kings had the right to keep such tortoises.

4 The prime minister of Chu.

5 A minister of Qi.

6 Another minister of Qi.

何如?
子曰:“清矣。”
曰:“仁矣乎?”
曰:“未知,焉得仁?”

5.20

季文子三思而后行。子闻之,曰:“再,斯可矣。”

5.21

子曰:“宁武子,邦有道则知,邦无道则愚。其知可及也,其愚不可及也。”

5.25

子曰:“巧言令色足恭,左丘明耻之,丘亦耻之。匿怨而友其人,左丘明耻之,丘亦耻之。”

8.1

子曰:“泰伯,其可谓至德也已矣。三以天下让,民无得而称焉。”

8.18

子曰:“巍巍乎,舜禹之有天下也而不与焉!”

state. Again he said, 'The officials here are no better than Minister Cui Zi', whereupon he left again. What do you think of him?"

The Master said, "He was a man of integrity."

Zizhang asked, "But was he humane?"

The Master answered, "I don't know whether he is a humane person."

5.20 Ji Wenzi[1] always thought three times before taking action. When the Master heard about this, he commented, "Twice is enough."

5.21 The Master said, "Ning Wuzi[2] was intelligent when the Way prevailed in the country. He became 'stupid' when the Way no longer prevailed. Others could match him in intelligence, but no one could equal him in 'stupidity.'"

5.25 The Master said, "Flattery, hypocrisy and obsequiousness — these Zuo Qiuming[3] considered shameful. So do I. To hide one's hatred for someone and pretend friendliness — that Zuo Qiuming considered shameful. So do I."

8.1 The Master said, "Tai Bo[4] can be said to be a man of the highest virtue. Several times he gave up his claim to the throne (in favor of his younger brother Ji Li). The common people could not find an adequate expression to praise him."

8.18 The Master said, "How lofty Shun and Yu were! All under Heaven was theirs and yet this meant nothing to them."

---

1 A minister of Lu.

2 A minister of Wei.

3 A historian of Lu who was supposed to have written a history book named *Spring and Autumn*.

4 The great grand uncle of King Wen of the Zhou dynasty.

8.19

子曰:“大哉尧之为君也！巍巍乎，唯天为大，唯尧则之。荡荡乎，民无能名焉。巍巍乎其有成功也，焕乎其有文章！”

14.9

或问子产。子曰:“惠人也。”

问子西。曰:“彼哉！彼哉！”

问管仲。曰:“人也。夺伯氏骈邑三百，饭疏食，没齿无怨言。”

14.12

子路问成人。

子曰:“若臧武仲之知，公绰之不欲，卞庄子之勇，冉求之艺，文之以礼乐，亦可以为成人矣。”

曰:“今之成人者何必然？见利思义，见危授命，久要不忘平生之言，亦可以为成人矣。”

14.13

子问公叔文子于公明贾曰:“信乎夫子不言、不笑、不取乎？”

8.19 Confucius said, "What a great sovereign Yao[1] was!" Nothing is greater than Heaven. Yao alone took it upon himself to make Heaven his model. So great were his blessings that the people could find no word to praise him. How splendid his achievements! How brilliant his cultural accomplishments!"

14.9 Someone asked about Zi Chan. The Master said, "He was a generous man."

When asked about Zi Xi, he said, "Oh, that man, what can one say about him?"

Asked about Guan Zhong, the Master remarked, "He was a real genius. He took three hundred households from the fief of the Bo family (in the city of Pian) and caused him to live on coarse grain for the rest of his life, yet the latter never complained."

14.12 Zilu asked how to become an accomplished man.

The Master said, "If one is able to combine the wisdom of Zang Wu-zhong, the self-denial of Gongchuo, the courage of Bian Zhuangzi and the skills of Ranqiu and, having done all this, he is further refined by the rituals and music, then he may be considered an accomplished man."

And he added, "But nowadays, an accomplished man may not possess all these qualities. He who can think of righteousness when gains come his way, who is ready to give up his life in the face of danger, and does not forget his promises when confronted with difficult circumstances, can be considered an accomplished man."

14.13 The Master asked Gongming Jia about his master Gongshu

1 Yao was another ruler whom Confucius considered to be a sage.

公明贾对曰："以告者过也。夫子时然后言，人不厌其言；乐然后笑，人不厌其笑；义然后取，人不厌其取。"
子曰："其然？岂其然乎？"

14.15

子曰："晋文公谲（jué）而不正，齐桓公正而不谲。"

14.16

子路曰："桓公杀公子纠，召忽死之，管仲不死。"曰："未仁乎？"子曰："桓公九合诸侯，不以兵车，管仲之力也。如其仁！如其仁！"

14.17

子贡曰："管仲非仁者与？桓公杀公子纠，不能死，又相之。"子曰："管仲相桓公，霸诸侯，一匡天下，民到于今受其赐。微管仲，吾其

Wenzi[1] "Is it true that your master never spoke, laughed or took anything from others?"

Gongming Jia answered, "Whoever told you that got it entirely wrong. My master spoke only when it was necessary for him to do so, he laughed only when he was happy, and he took only what was his due. That is why people never got tired of him."

The Master said, "Is that so! Is it really so!"

14.15 The Master said, "Duke Wen of Jin was crafty and not upright. Duke Huan of Qi was upright and not crafty."[2]

14.16 Zilu said, "When Duke Huan killed (his elder brother) Prince Jin, Zhao Hu committed suicide while Guan Zhong did not. Wasn't he wanting in humaneness?"

The Master answered, "Duke Huan managed to forge an alliance with the feudal lords on several occasions. He did this without resort to force. He succeeded in doing this thanks to the advice of Guan Zhong. Such was the latter's humaneness, such was his humaneness."[3]

14.17 Zigong asked, "Wasn't Guan Zhong wanting in humaneness? When Duke Huan killed Prince Jin, Guan Zhong did not kill himself but lived on to become the Duke's chief minister."

The Master answered, "Guan Zhong assisted Duke Huan in gaining dominance over the feudal lords and in bringing order to all states under heaven. To this day, the common people continue to enjoy the benefits of his contribution. Were it not for Guan Zhong, we would still be wearing our hair unbound

1 A minister of Wei.

2 Both being head of alliance of states.

3 Both Zhao Hu and Guan Zhong used to serve Prince Jin.

被发左衽矣。岂若匹夫匹妇之为谅也，自经于沟渎而莫之知也。”

15.5

子曰:“无为而治者，其舜也与？夫何为哉？恭己正南面而已矣。”

15.26

子曰:“吾犹及史之阙文也，有马者借人乘之，今亡矣夫。”

16.12

齐景公有马千驷，死之日，民无德而称焉。伯夷叔齐饿死于首阳之下，民到于今称之。其斯之谓与？

18.1

微子去之，箕子为之奴，比干谏而死。孔子曰:“殷有三仁焉。”

18.8

逸民：伯夷、叔齐、虞仲、夷逸、朱张、柳下惠、少连。子曰:“不

and folding our robes to the left.[1] Surely we would not want him to be like the common men who, in their petty loyalty to their sovereign, committed suicide in a gully without anyone taking notice."

15.5 The Master said, "Nobody except Shun[2] could govern so efficiently without exertion. What did he do? Nothing except sitting reverently in his royal seat facing south."

15.26 The Master said, "I can still find certain ambiguities in historical documents. Those who had horses were supposed to allow others to use them. Such practices are extinct nowadays."

16.12 Duke Jing of Qi had a thousand chariots, but when he died, the people could not think of anything to praise him for. Bo Yi and Shu Qi starved to death at the foot of Shouyang Mountain, but the people have been praising them ever since. Is this not proof of what we have just said?"

18.1 (King Zhou was very tyrannical.) Viscount Wei left him. Viscount Ji was condemned by him to be a slave. Bi Gan lost his life for remonstrating with him. Confucius said, "In these three men, the Shang (Yin) Dynasty found role models of humaneness."[3]

18.8 Bo Yi, Shu Qi, Yu Zhong, Yi Yi, Zhu Zhang, Liuxia Hui and Shao Lian were men who eventually withdrew from mundane affairs.

1 Both styles were considered uncultured at the time.

2 Shun had appointed capable persons as his ministers so that he needn't busy himself with the routines of government.

3 Viscount Wei was the elder step-brother of Zhou, the last King of the Shang Dynasty. Viscount Ji was Zhou's uncle. He tried to persuade Zhou to refrain from despotic rule. When the latter rejected his advice, he managed to save his life by feigning madness but was made a slave.Viscount Wei escaped. Bi Gan, Zhou's uncle and his prime minister, also remonstrated with the tyrant, who not only rejected his advice but also had his heart extracted.

降其志，不辱其身，伯夷、叔齐与！”
谓“柳下惠、少连，降志辱身矣，言中伦，行中虑，其斯而已矣。”
谓“虞仲、夷逸，隐居放言，身中清，废中权。”
“我则异于是，无可无不可。”

20.1

尧曰：“咨！尔舜！天之历数在尔躬，允执其中。四海困穷，天禄永终。”

舜亦以命禹。

曰：“予小子履，敢用玄牡，敢昭告于皇皇后帝：有罪不敢赦。帝臣不蔽，简在帝心。朕躬有罪，无以万方；万方有罪，罪在朕躬。”

周有大赉（lài），善人是富。“虽有周亲，不如仁人。百姓有过，在予一人。”

谨权量，审法度，修废官，四方之政行焉。

The Master said, "Bo Yi and Shu Qi would not compromise their aspirations, nor disgrace their integrity. Liuxia Hui and Shao Lian compromised their aspirations and suffered disgrace. But their words were consistent with their status and their behavior prudent.That is all one can say about them. Yu Zhong and Yi Yi led the life of a recluse and spoke their minds freely. They kept their character unsullied and showed sound judgment in accepting their dismissal. I am different from them in that I don't think there is any rigid rule as to what one should or should not do."

20.1 Yao said, "Oh, Shun, it is ordained by Heaven that the succession is to fall on you. You are to follow the middle way. If the multitude within the Four Seas should ever fall into poverty and misery, the blessing which Heaven bestowed on you will end forever."

Shun spoke the same words to Yu when proclaiming him the successor.

King Tang of Shang said, "I, Lü, the little one, venture to offer a black bull and make this declaration to you, the great Lord of Heaven: I dare not pardon those who have transgressed. Nor do I conceal the performance of my ministers, on whom you have already passed judgment. If I am found guilty, please do not let the people of the ten thousand fiefs suffer because of me; if the people of the ten thousand fiefs transgress, the guilt is mine alone."

During the Zhou Dynasty, a great number of people were made fiefs and the good people became prosperous. King Wu said, "Although I have many relatives, I prefer the virtuous. If the common people make mistakes, the blame is on me alone."

Unify weights and measures, standardize laws and regulations,

兴灭国，继绝世，举逸民，天下之民归心焉。
所重：民、食、丧、祭。
宽则得众，信则民任焉。敏则有功，公则说。

§ 11.3　评古今之事

13.7

子曰："鲁、卫之政，兄弟也。"

16.1

季氏将伐颛臾（zhuān yú）。冉有、季路见于孔子曰："季氏将有事于颛臾。"

孔子曰："求！无乃尔是过与？夫颛臾，昔者先王以为东蒙主，且在城邦之中矣，是社稷之臣也。何以伐为？"

and reestablish official posts which have been abolished, then government orders will be carried out throughout the country. Restore states which have been destroyed, revive lineages of big families which have become extinct, promote talents who have withdrawn from society and the hearts of all the common people under Heaven will turn to you.
Great attention should be paid to the common people's food supply and funeral and sacrificial rituals.
Tolerance gains the support of the multitude. Good faith wins the trust of the common people. Industriousness leads to success. Impartiality brings joy.

§ 11.3 About current and historical events.

13.7 The Master said, "In terms of government, the states of Lu and Wei are like brothers."[1]

16.1 The head of the Jisun Family was about to invade the principality of Zhuan Yu. Ranyou and Zilu, who were serving as stewards for the Jisun Family, came to see Confucius and said to him, "Our lord is planning an operation against Zhuan Yu."
Confucius said, "Ranyou, isn't this your fault? Formerly, the King of Zhou delegated to Zhuan Yu the right to conduct the sacrifice to Dongmeng Mountain. Lying within Lu's boundary, the Mountain is crucial to Lu's security. What right has your lord to attack it?"

1 When these two states were established, their founders were both sons of King Wen of Zhou.

冉有曰:“夫子欲之，吾二臣者皆不欲也。”

孔子曰:“求！周任有言曰:‘陈力就列，不能者止。’危而不持，颠而不扶，则将焉用彼相矣？且尔言过矣，虎兕（sì）出于柙（xiá），龟玉毁于椟中，是谁之过与？”

冉有曰:“今夫颛臾，固而近于费。今不取，后世必为子孙忧。”

孔子曰:“求！君子疾夫舍曰欲之而必为之辞。丘也闻有国有家者，不患寡而患不均，不患贫而患不安。盖均无贫，和无寡，安无倾。夫如是，故远人不服，则修文德以来之。既来之，则安之。今由与求也，相夫子，远人不服而不能来也，邦分崩离析而不能守也；而谋动干戈于邦内。吾恐季孙之忧，不在颛臾，而在萧墙之内也。”

Ranyou said, "Our lord insists that we invade it. Neither of us favor the move."
Confucius said, "Ranyou, there is a saying of Zhou Ren[1] which goes: 'Those who are ready to play their role stay in the rank; those who are not had better get out.' What is the use of a helper to a blind man if he cannot support him when he trips or falls. Besides, what you said is incorrect. Is no one responsible when a tiger or a rhino escapes from its cage, or when tortoise shells and jade are damaged in the casket?"
Ranyou said, "Zhuan Yu is heavily fortified and it is close to Fei[2]. If we do not seize it now, it will surely become a threat to Jisun's descendants."
Confucius said, "Ranyou, a man of honor detests those who use pretexts to cover up their avarice. I have heard it said that what the head of a state or a noble family should worry about is not the lack of people but the uneven distribution of wealth, not poverty but the lack of stability. So long as there is even distribution, the common people will not feel the poverty. So long as there is stability, the common people will not worry about the scarcity of people. So long as there is stability, the government will not be threatened by disintegration. If, in such circumstances, the distant people still refuse to conform, you need only promote your own culture and virtue to attract them; once they have come, you should let them feel contented. However, you two, as stewards, have failed to attract distant people or preserve the state when it faces disintegration. Instead, you propose to use force within the state. I am afraid Jisun's troubles lie not in Zhuan

1 A historian.
2 A fief of the Jisun Family.

16.3

孔子曰:“禄之去公室五世矣，政逮于大夫四世矣，故夫三桓之子孙微矣。”

Yu but within his palatial walls."

16.3 Confucius said, "The ducal house of Lu has lost control of its revenues for five generations. The Three Lords, too, have lost control of this matter for four generations. For this reason, their descendants are going downhill."

十二

孔子自评及处世之道

XII

Confucius' comments about himself and how he behaved in different situations

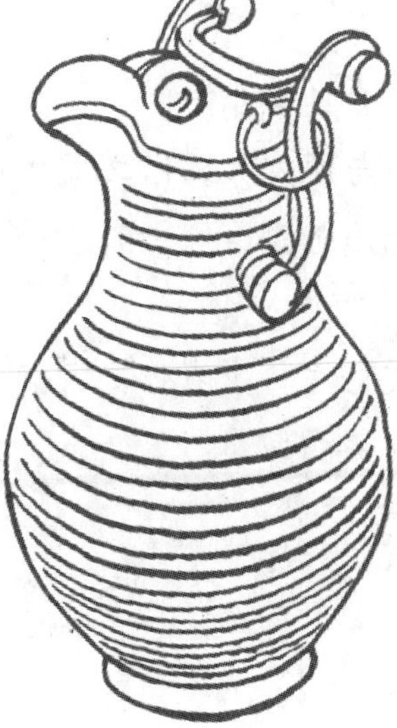

§12.1 孔子自评

2.4

子曰："吾十有五而志于学，三十而立，四十而不惑，五十而知天命，六十而耳顺，七十而从心所欲，不逾矩。"

2.21

或谓孔子曰："子奚不为政？"

子曰："《书》云：'孝乎惟孝，友于兄弟，施于有政。'是亦为政，奚其为为政？"

5.7

子曰："道不行，乘桴（fū）浮于海，从我者。其由与？"

子路闻之喜。子曰："由也好勇过我，无所取材。"

5.26

颜渊、季路侍。子曰："盍各言尔志。"

子路曰："愿车马衣轻裘与朋友共，敝之而无憾。"

颜渊曰："愿无伐善，无施劳。"

子路曰："愿闻子之志。"

子曰："老者安之，朋友信之，少者怀之。"

§ 12.1 About himself.

2.4 The Master said, "When I reached 15, I began devoting myself to learning. At 30, I could stand on my own. At 40, my mind was no longer confused. At 50, I knew what Heaven demanded of me. At 60, I was able to distinguish right from wrong in what other people told me. And since 70, I have been able to follow my heart's desire without transgressing rules."

2.21 Asked why he had not become involved in government, the Master answered, "The *Book of Historical Documents* says, 'Piety means being filial to your parents and being fraternal to your brothers; spreading this idea will exert an influence upon the government.' If that is so, why must I take part in government?"

5.7 The Master said, "If the Way should fail to prevail, I would let myself drift on the sea aboard a raft and the only one to accompany me would be Zilu." On hearing this, Zilu was overjoyed. The Master then said, "Zilu's courage far surpasses mine, but he can't find the wood to build the raft.

5.26 Yan Hui and Zilu were with Confucius when he said, "Now tell me what you wish for most."

Zilu said, "I wish to share with my friends my carriages and horses, my clothes and furs, and never complain even if they spoil them."

Yan Hui said, "I wish never to boast of my merits or show off what I have done."

Zilu asked the Master, "What is your fondest wish?"

Confucius said, "I wish for the old to live in peace and comfort, for friends to trust each other, and for the young to be taken

5.28

子曰:“十室之邑，必有忠信如丘者焉，不如丘之好学也。”

7.1

子曰:“述而不作，信而好古，窃比于我老彭。”

7.3

子曰:“德之不修，学之不讲，闻义不能徙，不善不能改，是吾忧也。”

7.5

子曰:“甚矣吾衰也！久矣吾不复梦见周公。”

7.6

子曰:“志于道，据于德，依于仁，游于艺。”

7.11

子谓颜渊曰:“用之则行，舍之则藏，惟我与尔有是夫！”

子路曰:“子行三军，则谁与？”

子曰:“暴虎冯河，死而无悔者，吾不与也。必也临事而惧。好谋而成者也。”

care of."

5.28 The Master said, "In a small village of ten families, there are bound to be honest and trust worthy people like me, but I don't think you will find anyone as eager to learn as I am."

7.1 The Master said, "I transmit but do not create. I'm a believer in and an admirer of the ancients. In my mind, I compare myself to Lao Peng[1].

7.3 The Master said, "Failure to cultivate virtue and review what I have learned, inability to practice what I have been told to be righteous and unwillingness to correct my mistakes—these are what worries me."

7.5 The Master said, "How I have aged! It has been a long time since I dreamed of the Duke of Zhou[2]."

7.6 The Master said, "I set my mind on the Way, persist in virtue, rely upon humaneness and delight in the arts."

7.11 The Master said to Yan Hui, "Only you and I are able to advance when called upon but prefer to stay in the background when neglected."

Zilu asked, "If you were to lead a grand army, whom would you like to take along with you?"

The Master answered, "I would not take along with me someone who would wrestle with a tiger with bare hands, or try to ford a river and die without regret. Instead, I would want someone who was thoughtful, cautious and capable of realizing his goal

---

1 Commentators differ as to whether "Lao Peng" refers to one person or two persons.

2 The Duke of Zhou was the brother of King Wu. Tradition had it that he established the rituals and regulations of the time. He was therefore greatly admired by Confucius.

7.12

子曰:“富而可求也;虽执鞭之士,吾亦为之。如不可求,从吾所好。”

7.16

子曰:“饭疏食饮水,曲肱而枕之,乐亦在其中矣。不义而富且贵,于我如浮云。”

7.17

子曰:“加我数年,五十以学《易》,可以无大过矣。”

7.19

叶(shè)公问孔子于子路,子路不对。子曰:“女奚不曰,其为人也,发愤忘食,乐以忘忧,不知老之将至云尔。”

7.20

子曰:“我非生而知之者,好古,敏以求之者也。”

7.22

子曰:“三人行,必有我师焉。择其善者而从之,其不善者而改之。”

7.23

子曰:“天生德于予,桓魋(tuí)其如予何?”

by strategy."

7.12 The Master said, "If wealth were an acceptable goal, then I wouldn't mind being a whip-holding guard for the marketplace. If it weren't, I'd rather follow my own inclination."[1]

7.16 The Master said, "There is joy in eating coarse grain, drinking plain water and using my elbow for a pillow. To me, riches and honors attained immorally are mere drifting clouds."

7.17 The Master said, "Let me live a few more years so that I may, at fifty, study the *Book of Changes*. Then I shall manage to avoid making serious mistakes."

7.19 When the Lord of She[2] asked Zilu about Confucius, Zilu failed to give him an answer. Later the Master said to Zilu, "Why didn't you say something like this: He is the sort of person who is so immersed in his studies that he forgets his meals, who is so happy that he forgets his worries, and who knows not the approach of old age."

7.20 The Master said, "I was not born with knowledge, but being an admirer of antiquity, I was eager to acquire knowledge about it."

7.22 The Master said, "Walking in the company of others, there is bound to be something I can learn from them. Their good traits I follow; their bad ones I try to avoid."

7.23 The Master said, "Heaven bestowed virtue on me, what can Huan Tui do to me?"[3]

1 Being a whip-holding guard for the marketplace was considered a lowly job in ancient China.

2 A minister of the State of Chu.

3 Huan Tui was a general of Song who attempted to kill Confucius.

7.24

子曰:“二三子以我为隐乎?吾无隐乎尔。吾无行而不与二三子者,是丘也。”

7.28

子曰:“盖有不知而作之者,我无是也。多闻,择其善者而从之,多见而识之,知之次也。”

7.33

子曰:“文,莫吾犹人也。躬行君子,则吾未之有得。”

7.34

子曰:“若圣与仁,则吾岂敢?抑为之不厌,诲人不倦,则可谓云尔已矣。”公西华曰:“正唯弟子不能学也。”

7.36

子曰:“奢则不孙,俭则固。与其不孙也,宁固。”

9.2

达巷党人曰:“大哉孔子!博学而无所成名。”子闻之,谓门弟子曰:“吾何执?执御乎?执射乎?吾执御矣。”

9.4

子绝四:毋意、毋必、毋固、毋我。

7.24 The Master said, "You, my pupils, do you think that I have kept something from you? No, there is nothing that I do which I don't share with you. That's me."

7.28 The Master said, "There are those who have innate knowledge, but I am not one of them. I listen to many views and choose the sound ones to follow. I see many things and keep them in my memory. Knowledge attained this way is the second best."[1]

7.33 The Master said, "In classics, I'm no worse than anyone else, but I have yet to become a man of honor who practices what he has learned."

7.34 The Master said, "How would I dare to consider myself a sage or a man of honor? Perhaps it can be said I tried unflaggingly to become one and to teach without growing weary, that is all." Gongxi Hua[2] said, "That is precisely what we disciples have not been able to emulate."

7.36 The Master said, "Extravagance leads to arrogance, and frugality to shabbiness. I would rather be shabby than arrogant."

9.2 A man from Daxiang village said, "Confucius is great indeed. He is learned, yet he has made no effort to make himself famous." When the Master heard this, he said to his disciples, "What shall I take up for my occupation? Chariot-driving or archery? I think I prefer chariot-driving."

9.4 The Master was free of four defects. He never made groundless speculation, did not claim absolute certainty, was not inflexible, and was not self-centered.

---

1 According to Confucius, innate knowledge is more reliable than his type of knowledge.

2 Confucius' disciple.

9.6

太宰问于子贡曰:“夫子圣者与? 何其多能也?” 子贡曰:“固天纵之将圣，又多能也。”

子闻之，曰:“太宰知我乎? 吾少也贱，故多能鄙事。君子多乎哉? 不多也。”

9.8

子曰:“吾有知乎哉? 无知也。有鄙夫问于我，空空如也。我叩其两端而竭焉。”

9.9

子曰:“凤鸟不至，河不出图，吾已矣夫!”

9.13

子贡曰:“有美玉于斯，韫匵（tuí）而藏诸? 求善贾而沽诸?” 子曰:“沽之哉，沽之哉! 我待贾者也。”

9.16

子曰:“出则事公卿，入则事父兄，丧事不敢不勉，不为酒困，何有于我哉?”

13.10

子曰:“苟有用我者，期月而已可也，三年有成。”

9.6 The Grand Minister asked Zigong, "Is your master a sage? If he is, why is he skilled in so many ways?" Zigong answered, "Precisely because Heaven has made him a sage, he is capable of many skills."

On hearing this, the Master said, "Does the Grand Master really know me? I was poor and humble when young. That's why I am skilled in so many menial skills. Would a man of honor need to master such skills? No, he needn't."

9.8 The Master said, "Am I a learned man? No, I am not. But if a farmer asks me a question and my mind is a total blank, I shall keep turning the question over in my mind until I come up with an answer."

9.9 The Master said, "The Phoenix does not appear. The River presents no chart. Alas! I am done for."[1]

9.13 Zigong asked, "Suppose you had a piece of beautiful jade, would you put it away in a safe, or would you sell it to one who knows its worth?" The Master said, "I would sell it! Yes, sell it! I'm just waiting for the right buyer."[2]

9.16 The Master said, "Serve the high officials in public life, tend to the elders at home, spare no effort in funeral arrangements and not be overcome by drinking—which of these are not within my ability?"

13.10 The Master said, "If someone had employed me, I would have brought things to a satisfactory state in a year's time; and in

---

1 Legend had it that when the phoenix appeared and a chart be afloat on the river, a golden age would come.

2 Confucius and Zigong were using beautiful jade as a metaphor for talented people. This passage shows how eager Confucius was for an official post to carry out his political program.

13.14

冉子退朝。子曰:“何晏也?”

对曰:“有政。”

子曰:“其事也?如有政,虽不吾以,吾其与闻之。”

14.35

子曰:“莫我知也夫!”

子贡曰:“何为其莫知子也?”

子曰:“不怨天,不尤人。下学而上达,知我者其天乎!”

14.39

子击磬于卫,有荷蒉(kuì)而过孔氏之门者,曰:“有心哉,击磬乎!”既而曰:“鄙哉!硁硁(kēng)乎!莫己知也,斯己而已矣。‘深则厉,浅则揭’。”

子曰:“果哉!末之难矣。”

15.3

子曰:“赐也!女以予为多学而识之者与?”对曰:“然,非与?”曰:“非也。予一以贯之。”

15.25

子曰:“吾之于人也,谁毁谁誉?”如有所誉者,其有所试矣。斯民也,

three years, I should have achieved wonderful results."

13.14 Ranyou returned from the court. The Master asked, "Why so late?" Ranyou replied, "There were state affairs to attend to."
The Master said, "They could only have been routine matters. Were they affairs of state, I would have heard about them, even though I am no longer in office."

14.35 The Master said, "Alas, it seems that no one understands me." Zigong asked why this was so.
The Master said, "I bear no grudges against Heaven or men. I learn what is common knowledge but reach upward to the ways of Heaven. Perhaps Heaven alone understands me."

14.39 Once, the Master was playing the stone chimes in the state of Wei. A man carrying some baskets happened to pass by his door. He said, "The man playing the stone chimes seems to be deeply troubled in his mind."
Presently, he added, "How mean this stubborn sound is. If the world continues to ignore you, so be it. 'Where the river is deep, wade across; where it is shallow, lift your gown (to keep it dry).'[1]"
The Master said, "With such resolution, nothing is too difficult to handle."

15.3 The Master said, "Zigong, do you think that I am a man with a wide range of knowledge and a good memory?" "Yes, I do, but isn't it so?" The Master said, "No. I have one single thread with which to bind together everything I know."

15.25 The Master said, "In dealing with the people around me, whom have I censured and whom have I praised? If I praised anyone, it

1 From the *Book of Songs*.

三代之所以直道而行也。”

§12.2　处世之道

3.17

子贡欲去告朔之饩（xì）羊。子曰：“赐也！尔爱其羊，我爱其礼。”

3.18

子曰：“事君尽礼，人以为谄也。”

5.7

子曰：“道不行，乘桴（fū）浮于海。从我者，其由与？”

子路闻之喜。子曰：“由也好勇过我，无所取材。”

6.28

子见南子，子路不说。夫子矢之曰：“予所否者，无厌之！天厌之！”

7.4

子之燕居，申申如也，夭夭如也。

was because his deeds had been put to test. The common people of the three dynasties (Xia, Shang and Zhou) followed the same principle, and that was why they kept to the Way."

§ 12.2 How he behaved in different situations.

3.17 Zigong wanted to do away with the offering of a live sheep during the sacrificial ceremony held on the first day of the Moon. The Master said, "Oh, Zigong! What you care for is the sheep, what I hold dear are the rituals."

3.18 The Master said, "In serving the ruler, I stick to the rituals, but this is regarded as currying favor with him."

5.7 The Master said, "If the Way should fail to prevail, I would let myself drift on the sea aboard a raft and the only one to accompany me would be Zilu." On hearing this, Zilu was overjoyed. The Master then said, "Zilu's courage far surpasses mine, but he can't find the wood to build the raft."

6.28 The Master called on Nan Zi[1]. Zilu was unhappy about the visit. The Master swore, "If I have done anything improper, may Heaven reject me! May Heaven reject me!"[2]

7.4 During his moments of leisure at home, the Master appeared relaxed and cheerful.

1 The consort of Duke Ling of Wei.

2 Nan Zi had a bad reputation because she was said to be lascivious and had undue influence in the Wei court.

7.9

子食于有丧者之侧，未尝饱也。

7.10

子于是日哭，则不歌。

7.13

子之所慎：齐、战、疾。

7.18

子所雅言，《诗》、《书》、执礼，皆雅言也。

7.27

子钓而不纲，弋不射宿。

7.31

陈司败问："昭公知礼乎？"孔子曰："知礼。"

孔子退，揖巫马期而进之，曰："吾闻君子不党，君子亦党乎？君取于吴，为同姓，谓之吴孟子。君而知礼，孰不知礼？"

巫马期以告。子曰："丘也幸，苟有过，人必知之。"

7.38

子温而厉，威而不猛，恭而安。

7.9 The Master would never eat his fill by the side of a mourner.

7.10 If Confucius had wept at a funereal, he would not sing for the rest of the day.

7.13 The Master was cautious when dealing with three matters: fasting before offering sacrifice, war and illness.

7.18 The Master used the Yayan when reciting the *Book of Songs* and the *Book of Records* or performing the rituals.[1]

7.27 The Master fished with a line but never with a net. He used corded arrows to shoot birds but never a roosting one.

7.31 The Minister of Justice of the State of Chen asked whether Duke Zhao of Lu knew the rituals. Confucius answered, "Yes, he does."

After Confucius had left, Chen approached Wuma Qi[2] and greeted him, saying, "It is said that a man of honor is never partial, but it seems to me that some men of honor are. The Duke took a lady from the State of Wu as his wife even though she had the same clan name as his and renamed her Wu Mengzi. If the Duke knew the rituals, who doesn't?"

When Wuma Qi passed on this comment to Confucius, the Master said, "How fortunate I am! Whenever I make a mistake, others are sure to notice it."

7.38 The Master was stern but cordial, awe-inspiring but not overbearing, dignified but easy to approach.

---

1 As the language used in the capital of Zhou, Yayan was the lingua franca of the Zhou Dynasty. Yayan was different from the various dialects used in Lu and other states. Ordinarily, Confucius spoke in the dialect of Lu.

2 Confucius' disciple.

9.10

子见齐衰（zī cuī）者、冕衣裳者与瞽（gǔ）者，见之，虽少，必作；过之，必趋。

9.12

子疾病，子路使门人为臣。病间，曰："久矣哉，由之行诈也。无臣而为有臣。吾谁欺？欺天乎？且予与其死于臣之手也，无宁死于二三子之手乎？且予纵不得大葬，予死于道路乎？"

9.14

子欲居九夷。或曰："陋，如之何？"子曰："君子居之，何陋之有？"

10.1

孔子于乡党，恂恂(xù)如也，似不能言者。其在宗庙、朝廷，便便言，唯谨尔。

10.2

朝，与下大夫言，侃侃如也；与上大夫言，訚訚（yín）如也。君在，踧踖（cú jí）如也，与与如也。

10.3

君召使摈，色勃如也；足躩如也。揖所与立，左右手，衣前后，襜

9.10 When the Master saw people in mourning clothes or ceremonial robes, or when he saw a blind person, even if they were younger in age, he would rise. When walking past them, he would quicken his steps to show respect.

9.12 The Master was seriously ill. Zilu asked his fellow disciples to act as retainers in mourning as for a lord. When his condition improved, the Master said, "Zilu, this farce has lasted too long. I am not entitled to have these retainers. Whom are we trying to fool? Heaven? Besides, I would rather have you, my disciples, and not the retainers at my bedside when I die. I may not be given an elaborate funeral, but I would not be left to die by the wayside, would I?"[1]

9.14 The Master wanted to move and settle among the Nine Tribes of the East. Someone told him, "The place is pretty wild. How would you be able to cope?" The Master answered, "Can you still consider it wild once a man of honor settles down there?"

10.1 In his own village, Confucius appeared very respectful, as if at a loss for words. In the ancestral temple or at court, he spoke articulately but was selective of words.

10.2 At court, when conversing with junior ministers, he spoke freely and affably; when conversing with senior ministers, he spoke respectfully. In the presence of the sovereign, he showed reverence and uneasiness, and his steps became gentle.

10.3 Summoned by the sovereign to receive foreign guests, he looked solemn, and his legs moved briskly. He greeted those lined up

---

1 During Confucius' time, only ministers kept retainers in their house. Confucius, having retired from his official post, had no retainers. He, therefore, disapproved of Zilu's arrangement which he considered presumptuous.

(chān) 如也。趋进，翼如也。宾退，必复命曰:“宾不顾矣。”

10.4

入公门，鞠躬如也，如不容。立不中门，行不履阈 (yù)。
过位，色勃如也，足躩如也，其言似不足者。
摄齐 (zī) 升堂，鞠躬如也，屏气似不息者。
出，降一等，逞颜色，怡怡如也。
没阶，趋进，翼如也。
复其位，踧踖如也。

10.5

执圭，鞠躬如也，如不胜。上如揖，下如授。勃如战色，足蹜蹜，如有循。享礼，有容色。

on both sides with his hands clasped, now to the left and now to the right; and his robes followed his movements without being disarranged. When he went forward (to greet the guests) with quickened steps, it seemed he was gliding on wings. When the guests had left, he invariably reported back to his sovereign, saying "The guests are out of sight."

10.4 On entering the gate of the duke's court, Confucius appeared uneasy and cautious as though there was little room for him there.

He dared not stand in the doorway, or tread on the threshold.

As he walked past where the ministers stood, he wore a solemn look and quickened his steps, speaking only in a soft tone.

When the audience began, he lifted the hem of his robe respectfully (as he ascended the steps) and it seemed he could hardly breathe.

Only when the audience had ended and he began to descend the steps did he breathe a sigh of relief and relax.

When he got to the bottom of the steps, he picked up speed as if on wings.

Once back in his place, he resumed his humble countenance.

10.5 (At the ceremony to meet a foreign mission), he bent his body slightly forward the jade tablet[1] seemed too heavy for him to carry. When he raised it with both hands, he seemed to be greeting; when he lowered it, he seemed ready to hand it to someone else. His solemn look gave the impression he was engaged in serious business. He walked with short steps along a single line.

---

1 A symbol of authority given to him by his sovereign.

私觌（dí），愉愉如也。

10.6

君子不以绀緅（gàn zōu）饰，红紫不以为亵服。

当暑，袗絺绤（zhěn chī xì），必表而出之。

缁衣，羔裘；素衣，麑（ní）裘；黄衣，狐裘。

亵裘（mè）长，短右袂。

必有寝衣，长一身有半。

狐貉之厚以居。

去丧，无所不佩。

非帷裳，必杀之。

羔裘玄冠不以吊。

吉月，必朝服而朝。

10.7

齐，必有明衣，布。

齐必变食，居必迁坐。

10.8

食不厌精，脍不厌细。

食饐（yì）而餲（ài），鱼馁而肉败，不食。色恶，不食。臭恶，不食。

When presenting the gifts, he looked amiable and courteous. When meeting in a private capacity with the hosts, he appeared relaxed and cheerful.

10.6 The man of honor (Confucius) does not use reddish black or dark grey for borders, nor red or violet for casual clothes.

In the heat of summer, he wears an unlined gown made of hemp or linen, making sure it covers the undergarment.

(In winter), he wears a black gown over a black lambskin, a white gown over a fawnskin robe and a yellow gown over yellow fox fur.

His informal fur coat is long but with a short right sleeve.

He requires his quilt to be one and half times his height.

Fox and raccoon pelts are used for cushions because their fur is thick.

He places no restrictions on the kind of ornament he wears once a period of mourning is over.

For non-ceremonial occasions, his gowns are made shorter.

Lambskin coats and black caps are not to be worn at funerals.

On the first day of the New Year, he invariably goes to the palace in full court attire.

10.7 In period of fasting, he invariably wears a cotton bathrobe. He also changes to a more simple diet and lives by himself.

10.8 (To Confucius) rice could never be over-husked and meat could never be too finely cut.

He did not eat staple food which had gone bad or fish and meat which had spoiled. He did not eat food whose color had changed or which had a bad smell. He did not touch food which was not properly prepared or when it was not the season for eating it. He

失饪，不食。不时，不食，割不正，不食。不得其酱，不食。肉虽多，不使胜食气。

唯酒无量，不及乱。

沽酒市脯，不食。

不撤姜食，不多食。

10.9

祭于公，不宿肉，祭肉不出三日。出三日，不食之矣。

10.10

食不语，寝不言。

10.11

虽疏食、菜羹、瓜祭，必齐如也。

10.12

席不正，不坐。

10.13

乡人饮酒，杖者出，斯出矣。

10.14

乡人傩（nuó），朝服而立于阼（zuò）阶。

did not eat meat which had not been slaughtered properly, or served without the proper sauce.

Even when there was plenty of meat, he avoided eating more meat than grain.

Only in drinking, he did not set himself a limit, but he never allowed himself to become drunk.

He did not touch wine or dried meat bought from the market.

Ginger he took at the end of each meal, but not in great amount.

10.9 When assisting at a sacrificial ceremony with the sovereign, he would not keep his portion of the sacrificial meat overnight. In other cases, he would not keep the sacrificial meat for more than three days. Beyond three days, he would not touch it.[1]

10.10 He would not converse during meals, nor would he talk before retiring for the night.

10.11 Even if his meal consisted of only coarse grain and vegetable soup, he would offer a sacrifice at each meal, with the same solemnity as during fasting.

10.12 He would not sit unless the mat was set properly.

10.13 When drinking at a village gathering, he would not leave until those with walking sticks[2] had done so.

10.14 When an exorcism was performed in his village, he would attend in his court robe standing on the steps facing east (where the host usually stood to welcome his guests).

1 In ancient times, the ministers accompanied the sovereign at sacrificial ceremonies, after which they would be granted a piece of sacrificial meat. As the ceremonies usually lasted two days, it would be at least more than three days if and when they ate the meat.

2 Referring to the elderly.

10.15

问人于他邦，再拜而送之。

10.16

康子馈药，拜而受之。曰:“丘未达，不敢尝。”

10.17

厩焚。子退朝，曰:“伤人乎?”不问马。

10.18

君赐食，必正席先尝之。君赐腥，必熟而荐之。君赐生，必畜之。侍食于君，君祭，先饭。

10.19

疾，君视之，东首，加朝服，拖绅。

10.20

君命召，不俟驾行矣。

10.21

入太庙，每事问。(同 **3.15**)

10.22

朋友死，无所归，曰:“于我殡。”

10.23

朋友之馈，虽车马，非祭肉，不拜。

10.15 When asking someone to extend his respects to a friend in another state, he would bow deeply twice, before sending him off.[1]

10.16 When presented with some medicine by Ji Kangzi, the Master accepted it with a deep bow. However, he said, "Not knowing its effects, I dare not try it."

10.17 The stable caught fire. Hurrying back from the court, the Master asked, "Was anyone hurt?" He did not ask about the horses.

10.18 When the sovereign granted him some cooked food, he would set his mat straight and taste the food immediately. When granted uncooked meat, he would first cook it and offer it to his ancestors. When granted a live animal, he would rear it. When accompanying the sovereign at a meal, he would eat only the rice while the sovereign performed the sacrificial offering.

10.19 When he was ill and the sovereign went to see him, Confucius made sure to lie with his head to the east[2] with his court robe draped over him (to show his respect) the sash dangling.

10.20 When the sovereign summoned him, he would set off on foot without waiting for his carriage to be yoked.

10.21 When he went inside the Grand Temple, he inquired about everything. (The same passage appeared in ***3.15***)

10.22 When a friend died and there was no kin to take care of his funeral service, the Master would say, "Leave it to me."

10.23 He would not bow when accepting gifts from a friend, even

1 One of the bows being meant for his friend.

2 The direction from which the sovereign would enter.

10.24

寝不尸，居不客。

10.25

见齐衰（zī cuī）者，虽狎，必变。见冕者与瞽者，虽亵，必以貌。
凶服者式之。式负版者。
有盛馔，必变色而作。
迅雷风烈必变。

10.26

升车，必正立，执绥。
车中，不内顾，不疾言，不亲指。

10.27

色斯举矣，翔而后集。曰："山梁雌雉，时哉时哉！"子路共之，三嗅而作。

if they were carriages and horses, the only exception being sacrificial meat.

10.24 When he slept, he did not lie flat on his back like a corpse. When alone at home, he did not sit as he would receiving a guest.

10.25 When he saw someone in mourning, whether the person was a close friend or not, he would change his expression to show sympathy. When he saw someone wearing a ceremonial cap or someone blind, even if it were a casual meeting, he would show respect.

On passing someone carrying costume for the dead, he would lean forward with his hands on the cross bar by way of showing respect. He would act in a similar manner toward someone carrying official documents.

When a sumptuous feast was brought in, his face would assume a solemn expression and he would rise to his feet.

His countenance would change with a clap of thunder or a strong gust of wind.

10.26 When mounting a carriage, he would first stand upright and hold on to the hand rail to pull himself up.

Once in his seat, he would not look inside the carriage, nor talk volubly, nor point his fingers around.

10.27 (Confucius and Zilu came upon some pheasants.) The Master's face lit up. Startled, the birds took flight. They circled for a while before alighting. Confucius exclaimed, "Pheasants on the mountain ridge! It is the season! It is the season!" Zilu cupped one hand in the other (in a symbol of respect), but the pheasants

11.8

颜渊死，颜路请子之车以为之椁（guǒ）。子曰：“才不才，亦各言其子也。鲤也死，有棺而无椁。吾不徒行以为之椁。以吾从大夫之后，不可徒行也。”

11.11

颜渊死，门人欲厚葬之，子曰：“不可。”

门人厚葬之。子曰：“回也视予犹父也，予不得视犹子也。非我也，夫二三子也。”

14.21

陈成子弑简公。孔子沐浴而朝，告于哀公曰：“陈恒弑其君，请讨之。”

公曰：“告夫三子。”

孔子曰：“以吾从大夫之后，不敢不告也。君曰‘告夫三子’者。”

之三子告，不可。孔子曰：“以吾从大夫之后，不敢不告也。”

14.32

微生亩谓孔子曰：“丘，何为是栖栖者与？无乃为佞乎？”孔子曰：“非

flapped their wings three times and flew away.[1]

11.8 When Yan Hui died, (his father) Yan Lu asked the Master to sell his carriage in order to pay for an outer coffin for his son. The Master said, "Everyone speaks for his son, whether he is talented or not. When my son Li died, he had a coffin but no outer coffin. I could not go around on foot just in order to provide him with an outer coffin because it would be improper for me, a former official, to travel on foot."

11.11 When Yan Hui died, the disciples wanted to hold a grand funeral for him. The Master said, "You mustn't do that." All the same, the disciples went ahead and buried him in grand style. The Master said, "Hui, you treated me like I was your father, but I have not been able to treat you like a son. This is not my fault, but that of your fellow disciples."

14.21 Chen Hengzi killed Duke Jian (of Qi). After a ceremonial bath, Confucius went to the court of Lu and informed Duke Ai of the event. "Chen Hengzi has slain his sovereign," he said. "Please send an expeditionary force against him."The duke said, "Go and report to the Three Lords (Jisun, Zhongsun and Mengsun)." (After he had left the court,) Confucius said, "Because I was once a minister, I dared not leave the case unreported. Yet the sovereign asked me to 'report'to the Lords."He went and reported to the Three Lords, but they refused to take any action. Confucius repeated, "Because I was once a minister, I dared not leave the case unreported."

14.32 Weisheng Mu asked Confucius, "Why are you rushing about so?

1 Since ancient times, scholars have not been able to find a satisfactory explanation for the significance of this passage.

敢为佞也，疾固也。”

17.5

公山弗扰以费畔，召，子欲往。

子路不悦，曰:“末之也已，何必公山氏之之也。”

子曰:“夫召我者，而岂徒哉？如有用我者，吾其为东周乎？”

17.7

佛肸（bì xī）召，子欲往。

子路曰:“昔者由也闻诸夫子曰:‘亲于其身为不善者，君子不入也。’佛肸以中牟畔，子之往也，如之何？”

子曰:“然，有是言也。不曰坚乎，磨而不磷；不曰白乎，涅而不缁。吾岂匏瓜也哉？焉能系而不食？”

17.20

孺悲欲见孔子，孔子辞以疾。将命者出户，取瑟而歌，使之闻之。

Aren't you showing off your clever tongue?" Confucius answered, "I'm not so impertinent as to show off anything. I merely detest those with incorrigible stubbornness."

17.5 Gongshan Furao took the city of Fei and used it as his stronghold to stage a revolt (against the Jisun Family). He summoned Confucius to join him. The Master was inclined to do so.
Zilu was unhappy about this, saying, "We may have nowhere else to go, but must we really go and see Gongshan?"
The Master answered, "Do you think the man is summoning me for no reason at all? Should I get a post there, could I not establish a 'Zhou in the east'?"[1]

17.7 When Bi Xi summoned Confucius, the Master intended to go. Zilu said, "Master, I remember hearing from you that the man of honor does not associate with those who have committed evil. Now Bi Xi is entrenched in Zhongmo, ready to stage a revolt. Yet you are thinking of joining him. How can you justify yourself?" Confucius said, "Indeed, I did say that, yet 'what is really hard can never be worn thin; what is pure white can never be dyed black'[2]. Am I just a gourd good enough for decoration but is not edible?"[3]

17.20 Ru Bei wanted to see Confucius, but the latter declined on grounds of illness. As soon as the messenger stepped out of the door, Confucius picked up his lute and began to sing, making sure that

1 Confucius considered the Western Zhou Dynasty, especially during the reign of King Wu and his son assisted by his uncle Lord Zhou, as the ideal society. The state of Lu was to the east of the Zhou capital .

2 From the *Book of Songs*.

3 A figure of speech implying that Confucius hoped to secure an official position to carry out his political program.

18.3

齐景公待孔子曰："若季氏，则吾不能；以季、孟之间待之。"曰："吾老矣，不能用也。"孔子行。

18.4

齐人归女乐，季桓子受之，三日不朝。孔子行。

Ru Bei heard it.

18.3 Asked how he would treat Confucius, Duke Jing of Qi said, "I am unable to accord him the treatment that the Jisun Family received (from his duke), so I shall place him somewhere between Jisun and Mengsun." "I am getting old," he explained, "I shall not be able to make use of his talents." Whereupon Confucius departed from Qi.

18.4 The State of Qi sent a group of sing-song girls to the State of Lu. Ji Huanzi[1] accepted them and, for many days afterwards, he stayed away from court. Whereupon Confucius departed from Lu.

1 The Chief Minister of Lu.

十三

孔子的弟子

XIII

Confucius' Disciples

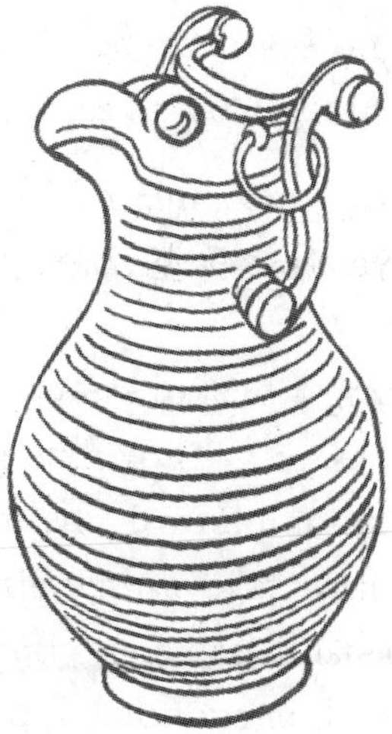

§13.1 生前评说

1.10

子禽问于子贡曰：夫子至于是邦也，必闻其政，求之与，抑与之与？”子贡曰：“夫子温、良、恭、俭、让以得之。夫子之求之也，其诸异乎人之求之与？”

3.24

仪封人请见，曰：“君子之至于斯也，吾未尝不得见也。”从者见之。出曰：“二三子何患于丧乎？天下之无道也久矣，天将以夫子为木铎。”

9.7

牢曰：“子云：‘吾不试，故艺’。”

9.11

颜渊喟然叹曰：“仰之弥高，钻之弥坚，瞻之在前，忽焉在后。夫子

§ 13.1 What they said about Confucius during his lifetime.

1.10 Chen Kang[1] asked Zigong[2], "When our Master goes to another state, he is always able to learn a good deal about how it is governed. Does he go about seeking such information or do people there just give it to him of their own accord?"

Zigong answered, "Our Master gets the information he needs because he is temperate, kind, courteous, restrained and magnanimous. Our Master's way of gathering information is quite unique, isn't it?"

3.24 An officer in the border region of Yi requested an audience with Confucius, saying, "I have never failed to meet with men of honor who have come my way." The disciples then presented him to the Master.

When he came out, he told them, "Don't you worry about him not having an official post. The world has long lost the Way. Heaven is about to use your master as a wooden bell to arouse the people."

9.7 Zi lao[3] quoted the Master as saying, "Because I have not taken up any official post, I have to learn so many different arts."

9.11 Yan Hui said with a sigh, "The more I look up to the Master's teachings, the more lofty they seem to be. The more I delve into them, the more profound they become. I see them before me,

---

1 Confucius' disciple, also known as Ziqin.

2 Confucius' disciple, also known as Duanmu Ci.

3 Considered by some commentators as having studied under Confucius.

循循然善诱人，博我以文，约我以礼，欲罢不能。即竭吾才，如有所立，卓尔。虽欲从之，末由也已。”

11.23

子畏于匡，颜渊后。子曰:“吾以女为死矣。”

曰:“子在，回何敢死?”

14.28

子曰:“君子道者三，我无能焉；仁者不忧，知者不惑，勇者不惧。”

子贡曰:“夫子自道也。”

§ 13.2　逝后评说

19.22

卫公孙朝问于子贡曰:“仲尼焉学?”

子贡曰:“文武之道，未坠于地，在人。贤者识其大者，不贤者识其小者，莫不有文武之道焉。夫子焉不学? 而亦何常师之有?”

suddenly they are behind me. The Master is adept at leading me on step by step. He has broadened my mind with knowledge and restrained me with the rituals. I could not give up my studies even if I wanted to. Having exerted myself to the best of my ability, I seem to have made some achievement, but to go further, I am still at a loss."

11.23 The Master was besieged at Kuang. Yan Hui fell behind. When he arrived, Confucius said, "I thought you were dead."
To which Yan Hui replied, "How would I dare to die when you, my Master, are still alive."

14.28 The Master said, "The Way of the man of honor contains three principles, none of which I have been able to accomplish. Being humane, he has no worries; being wise, he is not confused and being courageous, he does not fear."
Zigong commented, "That is just a modest way by which the Master describes himself."

§ 13.2 What they said about Confucius after his death.

19.22 Gongsun Chao of the State of Wei asked Zigong from whom did Confucius acquire his learning.
Zigong answered, "The Way of King Wen and King Wu (of the Zhou Dynasty) is not lost. It can be found among the people. The virtuous grasps its essence while the mediocre grasps the details. The Way of King Wen and Wu is omnipresent. Where can't my Master learn? Where is the need for him to have one

19.23

叔孙武叔语大夫于朝曰:“子贡贤于仲尼。”

子服景伯以告子贡。

子贡曰:“譬之宫墙,赐之墙也及肩,窥见室家之好。夫子之墙数仞,不得其门而入,不见宗庙之类,百官之富。得其门者或寡矣。夫子之云,不亦宜乎!”

19.24

叔孙武叔毁仲尼。子贡曰:“无以为也!仲尼不可毁也。他人之贤者,丘陵也,犹可逾也;仲尼,日月也,无得而逾焉。人虽欲自绝,其何伤于日月乎?多见其不知量也。”

19.25

陈子禽谓子贡曰:“子为恭也,仲尼岂贤于子乎?”

子贡曰:“君子一言以为知,一言以为不知,言不可不慎也。夫子之不可及也,犹天之不可阶而升也。夫子之得邦家者,所谓立之斯立,

specific teacher?"

19.23 Shusun Wushu[1] told his fellow officials in court, "Zigong is wiser than his Master."

Zifu Jingbo[2] reported this observation to Zigong.

Zigong said, "Let's take the outside wall of a house as a metaphor. My wall is at shoulder height, so that the fine architecture inside can be seen from without. My Master's wall is several scores of feet high. If one is unable to find the entrance, he cannot see the magnificence of the ancestral temples and the splendor of the mansions within. Since those who can find the entrance are at best a few, is it not understandable that your master should have spoken thus?"

19.24 Shusun Wushu slandered Confucius. Zigong said, "It will make no difference. Confucius is above slander. Other virtuous men are like low hills that can be surmounted. But Confucius is like the sun and the moon that are insurmountable. Even if someone wanted to alienate himself from them, that would not harm the sun and the moon one bit. It would only serve to show that he did not know his own measure."

19.25 Chen Ziqin said to Zigong, "Surely you are being respectful to Confucius. Do you really think he is superior to you?"

Zigong said, "A single utterance is enough to judge whether a man is wise or foolish. That is why one must be careful with his words. The Master cannot be equaled just as the sky cannot be reached by climbing a ladder. Were the Master to become the head of a state or of a noble family, he would have been able

1 A minister of Lu.

2 Also a minister of Lu.

道之斯行，绥之斯来，动之斯和。其生也荣，其死也哀，如之何其可及也？”

§13.3 解说孔子思想

16.13

陈亢问于伯鱼曰:“子亦有异闻乎？”

对曰:“未也。尝独立，鲤趋而过庭。曰:‘学诗乎？’对曰:‘未也’。‘不学诗，无以言。’鲤退而学诗。他日又独立，鲤趋而过庭。曰:‘学礼乎？’对曰:‘未也。’‘不学礼，无以立。’鲤退而学礼。闻斯二者。”

陈亢退而喜曰:“问一得三：闻诗，闻礼，又闻君子之远（yuàn）其子也。”

to accomplish what is described in the saying; 'He only has to raise them and they will stand up, to guide them and they will walk, to grant them peace and they will turn to him, to motivate them and they will work in harmony.' My Master deserves honor while alive. When he dies, he deserves to be mourned. How can he be equaled?"

§ 13.3 Their interpretations of Confucius' core ideas.

16.13 Chen Kang[1] asked Confucius' son, Bo Yu, "Have you received any special coaching from the Master?"

He replied, "No. One day, my father was standing alone. As I hurried to cross the courtyard, he asked me, 'Have you studied the *Book of Songs*?' I answered, 'No.' He said, 'Unless you have studied it, you won't know how to speak properly.' I retired to study the *Book of Songs*. Another day, my father was again standing alone and as I hurried across the courtyard, he asked again, 'Have you studied the *Book of Rites*?' When I said no, he said, 'Unless you have studied it, you won't know how to behave properly.' I retired to study the *Book of Rites*. These were the two things I learned from him."

Chen Kang went away delighted, saying "I merely asked one question. However, I managed to learn three things: about the *Book of Songs* about the *Book of Rites* and about how a man of honor keeps a distance from his son."

---

1 Confucius' disciple.

18.7

子路从而后，遇丈人，以杖荷蓧（diào）。

子路问曰:“子见夫子乎?”

丈人曰:“四体不勤，五谷不分，孰为夫子?”植其杖而芸。

子路拱而立。

止子路宿，杀鸡为黍而食（sì）之。见其二子焉。

明日，子路行以告。

子曰:“隐者也。”使子路反见之。至，则行矣。子路曰:“不仕无义。长幼之节，不可废也；君臣之义，如之何其废之?欲洁其身，而乱大伦。君子之仕也，行其义也。道之不行，已知之矣。”

19.2

子张曰:“执德不弘，信道不笃，焉能为有?焉能为亡?”

19.3

子夏之门人问交于子张。

子张曰:“子夏云何?”

对曰:“子夏曰:‘可者与之，其不可者拒之。’”

18.7 When accompanying Confucius on his travels, Zilu fell behind. He met an old man carrying a stick and a hoe on his shoulder.

Zilu asked, "Have you seen my Master?"

To which the old man replied, "What kind of a master is he if he does not use his four limbs and cannot tell one kind of grain from another?" He then planted his stick in the ground and went on weeding.

Zilu stood there respectfully.

The old man invited Zilu to stay for the night, slaughtered a chicken and prepared some millet for his guest to whom he also introduced his two sons.

The next day, Zilu caught up with Confucius and told him his experience.

The Master said, "He must be a recluse", and sent his student back to look for the old man. But when Zilu returned to the site, the old man had already left.

Zilu commented, "It is not right to refuse to take office. We cannot abandon the mutual obligations between seniors and juniors, still less those between the sovereign and his ministers. To keep one's virtue unsullied by withdrawing from the world is to cause confusion in the most fundamental human relationships. The man of honor takes office in order to perform his duty, knowing all along that the Way has not prevailed."

19.2 Zizhang said, "If a man is not steadfast in acting virtuously and forsakes his own beliefs, can it be said that he is dedicated or not?"

19.3 One of Zixia's disciples asked Zizhang about making friends.

Zizhang asked, "What has your master told you?"

The student answered, "Be friendly with good people and spurn

子张曰："异乎吾所闻：君子尊贤而容众，嘉善而矜不能。我之大贤与，于人何所不容？我之不贤与，人将拒我，如之何其拒人也？"

19.4

子夏曰："虽小道，必有可观者焉，致远恐泥，是以君子不为也。"

19.5

子夏曰："日知其所亡，月无忘其所能，可谓好学也已矣。"

19.6

子夏曰："博学而笃志，切问而近思，仁在其中矣。"

19.7

子夏曰："百工居肆以成其事，君子学以致其道。"

19.8

子夏曰："小人之过也必文。"

19.9

子夏曰："君子有三变：望之俨然，即之也温，听其言也厉。"

19.10

子夏曰："君子信而后劳其民；未信，则以为厉己也，信而后谏；未信，则以为谤己也。"

those who are not."

Zizhang said, "That's not what I was taught. I was taught that the man of honor respects the virtuous and tolerates the ordinary. He lauds the wise while sympathizing with the mediocre. If I am a truly virtuous man, why should I be intolerant of others? If I am not, then the others will spurn me, then how can I spurn them?"

19.4 Zixia said, "Even minor skills have their worth, but the man of honor with a long journey ahead does not engage in them for fear of being bogged down."

19.5 Zixia said, "He who is aware of the need to learn every day and reviews each month what he has learnt is truly fond of learning."

19.6 Zixia said, "Learn extensively, hold fast to your purpose and interest, pose questions in earnest and reflect on issues at hand, then humaneness is within reach."

19.7 Zixia said, "The artisans master their crafts by living in their workshops. The man of honor arrives at his Way through learning."

19.8 Zixia said, "The petty-minded man tries his best to cover up his errors."

19.9 Zixia said, "The man of honor leaves people with three different impressions: From a distance, he looks solemn; when close at hand, he is cordial; when he speaks, it is with a firm tone."

19.10 Zixia said, "The man of honor has first to win the trust of the common people before he can make them work. Otherwise, they will feel abused. He has first to win the confidence of the ruler before he can remonstrate with him, for without this confidence, the ruler might take it as an insult."

19.11

子夏曰:“大德不逾闲，小德出入可也。”

19.12

子游曰:“子夏之门人小子，当洒扫应对进退，则可矣，抑末也。本之则无，如之何?”

子夏闻之，曰:“噫，言游过矣！君子之道，孰先传焉? 孰后倦焉? 譬诸草木，区以别矣。君子之道，焉可诬也? 有始有卒者，其惟圣人乎?”

19.14

子游曰:“丧致乎哀而止。”

19.15

子游曰:“吾友张也，为难能也，然而未仁。”

19.16

曾子曰:“堂堂乎张也，难与并为仁矣。”

19.17

曾子曰:“吾闻诸夫子：人未有自致者也，必也亲丧乎。”

19.18

曾子曰:“吾闻诸夫子：孟庄子之孝也，其他可能也；其不改父之臣与父之政，是难能也。”

19.11 Zixia said, "One must not step out of bounds on matters concerning virtue. Transgressions on small matters are permissible."

19.12 Ziyou said, "The disciples and followers of Zixia can manage such trifles as sweeping and cleaning, and escorting and sending off guests. But when it comes to the basics[1], they have no idea. How can that be?"

When Zixia heard this, he said, "Alas, Ziyou has got it wrong. In teaching the Way of a man of honor, what is to be taught first and what last? It is like the classification of plants, which can only be done according to the specific features of each. How can one distort the way of the man of honor? It is probably a sage who alone can teach his disciples in the proper order from beginning to end."

19.14 Ziyou said, "When in mourning, one should not go beyond expressing grief."

19.15 Ziyou said, "My friend Zizhang is a rare talent. Still, he has not yet attained humaneness."

19.16 Master Zeng said, "Zizhang is such a great scholar that it is difficult to arrive at humaneness together with him."

19.17 Master Zeng said, "I once heard the Master say that it is only when mourning for one's parents does one fully reveal his emotions."

19.18 Master Zeng said, "I once heard my Master say, one may emulate Meng Zhuangzi's filial piety, but it will be difficult to follow his example of not removing his father's officials or changing his policies."

---

1 The rituals and music.

19.19

孟氏使阳肤为士师，问于曾子。曾子曰：“上失其道，民散久矣。如得其情，则哀矜而勿喜。”

19.20

子贡曰：“纣之不善，不如是之甚也。是以君子恶居下流，天下之恶皆归焉。”

19.21

子贡曰：“君子之过也，如日月之食焉。过也，人皆见之；更也，人皆仰之。”

§ 13.4 孔子评价弟子

1.15

子贡曰：“贫而无谄，富而无骄，何如？”

子曰：“可也。未若贫而乐，富而好礼者也。”

子贡曰：“《诗》云，‘如切如磋！如琢如磨’，其斯之谓与？”

19.19 The Mengsun family appointed Yang Fu judge. Yang Fu sought Master Zeng's advice. The latter said, "Those in authority have lost the Way and the common people have long lost faith in them and become disorganized. If you succeed in extracting the truth from the criminals, have pity on them and do not pat yourself on the back."

19.20 Zigong said, " Zhou (of Shang Dynasty) may not have been as bad a ruler as he was said to be. That is why those in authority are afraid of landing on the wrong side of history. Once they are in that situation, all the dirt of the world will be thrown on them."

19.21 Zigong said, "The man of honor's mistakes are like the eclipses of the sun and the moon. When he makes a mistake, everyone will notice it. When he corrects his mistake, he will be looked up to all the more."

§ 13.4 What Confucius said about his disciples and how he evaluated them.

1.15 Zigong asked, "What do you think of one who is poor without being obsequious, wealthy without being arrogant?"

The Master answered, "That is pretty good, but not as good as one who is poor yet cheerful, or one who is wealthy yet observant of regulations and rituals."

Zigong said, "In the *Book of Songs*, there are these lines: 'As bone

子曰：“赐也！始可与言《诗》已矣，告诸往而知来者。”

2.9

子曰：“吾与回言，终日不违，如愚。退而省其私，亦足以发，回也不愚。”

5.1

子谓公冶长，“可妻也。虽在缧绁（léi xiè）之中，非其罪也。”以其子妻之。

5.2

子谓南容，“邦有道，不废；邦无道，免于刑戮。”以其兄之子妻之。

5.3

子谓子贱，“君子哉若人！鲁无君子者，斯焉取斯？”

5.4

子贡问曰：“赐也何如？”

子曰：“女，器也。”

曰：“何器也？”

carved and polished, as jade cut and ground'. Is that what you meant?"

The Master said, "Oh, Zigong! Now I can discuss the *Book of Songs* with you. You know what is yet to come on the basis of what I have told you."

2.9 The Master said, "Hui[1] never disagrees with me even when we spend the whole day talking to each other. It would seem as though he were slow-witted. But later I found that when he is on his own, he is quite creative. Hui is actually not slow-witted at all."

5.1 The Master said of Gongye Chang[2], "He would make a good husband. He was innocent though he was once imprisoned." He then had his daughter marry Gongye Chang.

5.2 The Master said of Nan Rong[3], "When the Way prevails in the country, he is not cast aside. When it no longer prevails, he stays away from punishment." He then had his niece marry Nan Rong.

5.3 When talking about Zijian[4], the Master said, "Here is a man of honor. If there were no men of honor in the State of Lu, where could he have acquired such virtue?"

5.4 Zigong asked, "What do you think of me?"

To which the Master answered, "You are like a vessel."

"What kind of a vessel?"

1 Yan Hui, Confucius' disciple.

2 Confucius' disciple.

3 Confucius' disciple.

4 Confucius' disciple.

曰:“瑚琏也。”

5.5

或曰:“雍也仁而不佞（nìng）。”

子曰:“焉用佞？御人以口给，屡憎于人，不知其仁。焉用佞？”

5.6

子使漆雕开仕。对曰:“吾斯之未能信。”子说（yuè）。

5.8

孟武伯问子路仁乎？子曰:“不知也。”

又问。子曰:“由也，千乘之国，可使治其赋也，不知其仁也。”

“求也何如？”

子曰:“求也，千室之邑，百乘之家，可使为之宰也，不知其仁也。”

“赤也何如？”

子曰:“赤也，束带立于朝，可使与宾客言也，不知其仁也。”

5.9

子谓子贡曰:“女与回也孰愈？”

对曰:“赐也何敢望回？回也闻一以知十，赐也闻一以知二。”

子曰:“弗如也。吾与女弗如也。”

"Oh, a gemmed sacrificial vessel."[1]

5.5 Someone said, "Ran Yong is humane, but not eloquent."
The Master said, "What need is there for eloquence? He who is too clever in speech will be disliked by others. I cannot say whether Ran Yong is humane, but must he be eloquent?"

5.6 The Master wanted Qidiao Kai[2] to take an official post. But Qidiao Kai said, "I cannot trust myself to do so now." The Master was very pleased with his answer.

5.8 Meng Wubo asked whether Zilu was humane. The Master said, "I cannot say he is." Meng repeated his question. The Master said, "Zilu can manage the military affairs of a state of one thousand chariots, but I don't know if he is humane."
Meng asked about Ranqiu.
The Master answered, "Ranqiu can be the magistrate of a town with one thousand households or the steward of a noble's manor with a hundred chariots, but I don't know if he is humane."
Meng then asked about Gongxi Hua.
The Master answered, "Gongxi Hua is suitable for conversing with guests when he wears his saches and takes his place at court, but I don't know if he is humane."

5.9 The Master asked Zigong, "Who is wiser? You or Yan Hui?"
Zigong answered, "How dare I compare myself with Yan Hui? When he is taught one thing, he understands ten. When I am taught one thing, I understand two."
The Master said, "Indeed, you and I are no match for Yan Hui."

1 A vessel can only "serve one purpose", so here Confucius was implying that Zigong should work hard to become a man of honor who can serve different purposes, in short, an all-round person.

2 Confucius' disciple.

5.10

宰予昼寝，子曰:“朽木不可雕也，粪土之墙不可杇（wū）也，于予与何诛？”子曰:“始吾于人也，听其言而信其行；今吾于人也，听其言而观其行。于予与改是。”

5.11

子曰:“吾未见刚者。”

或对曰:“申枨（chéng）。”

子曰:“枨也欲，焉得刚？”

5.12

子贡曰:“我不欲人之加诸我也，吾亦欲无加诸人。”

子曰:“赐也，非尔所及也。”

5.14

子路有闻，未之能行，唯恐有闻。

5.22

子在陈，曰:“归与！归与！吾党之小子狂简，斐然成章，不知所以裁之。”

6.1

子曰:“雍也可使南面。”

5.10 Zai Yu (also known as Zaiwo) fell asleep during the day. The Master said, "One cannot carve on a piece of rotten wood, nor can one whitewash a wall of dried dung. What is the use of scolding a fellow like him?" He added, "I used to listen to what people say and trust that they would act accordingly. Now I listen to what people say and observe how they act. Zai Yu has made me change my attitude."

5.11 The Master said, "I have never met anyone who is truly unyielding." Someone suggested Sheng Cheng[1] was such a person.
The Master said, "He is driven by desires, how can he be unyielding?"

5.12 Zigong said, "I don't want to do to others what I don't want them to do to me."
The Master commented, "Zigong, you have yet to live up to that saying."

5.14 Zilu would not let himself be told anything new before he had put into practice what he had already learned.

5.22 When the Master was in the State of Chen, he said (to those who accompanied him), "Let's go home. Let's go home. My disciples at home are ambitious and already accomplished. I don't know how I could further refine them."

6.1 The Master said, "Oh, Ranyong[2], he could be given the seat facing south."[3]

---

1 Confucius's disciple.

2 Confucius' disciple.

3 In ancient China, the seat facing south was always reserved for the most respected person or persons in the room. People with high positions were seated southward. Here, Confucius was saying that Ranyong had the potential of becoming an important official.

6.3

哀公问:“弟子孰为好学?”

孔子对曰:“有颜回者好学,不迁怒,不贰过,不幸短命死矣。今也则亡,未闻好学者也。”

6.6

子谓仲弓,曰:“犁牛为之骍(xīn)且角。虽欲勿用,山川棒舍诸?”

6.7

子曰:“回也,其心三月不违仁,其余则日月至焉而已矣。”

6.8

季康子问:“仲由可使从政也与?”

子曰:“由也果,于从政乎何有?”

曰:“赐也可使从政也与?”

曰:“财也达,于从政乎何有?”

曰:“求也可使从政也与?”

曰:“求也艺,于从政乎何有?”

6.9

季氏使闵子骞为费宰,闵子骞曰:“善为我辞焉!如有复我者,则吾

6.3 Duke Ai of Lu asked of Confucius, "Who among your disciples truly loves learning?"

The Master answered, "There was Yan Hui. He loved to learn. He never vented his anger on others and he never made the same mistake. Unfortunately, he died young and now there is none. At least, I do not know of anyone who is so keen on learning."

6.6 The Master said of Ranyong, "Should there be a bull born of plough oxen have a coat of red hair and well-formed horns, would the God of Mountains and Rivers let it be cast aside, even if people feel it is not good enough for the ceremonial sacrifice?"[1]

6.7 The Master said, "No one but Yan Hui could focus his mind on humaneness for so long. The rest can attain such a state only occasionally."

6.8 Jikang Zi[2] asked, "Can Zilu be an official?"

The Master answered, "Zilu is resolute. There should be no difficulty for him to become an official."

The Minister then asked about Zigong .

The Master answered, "Zigong is intelligent. There should be no difficulty for him to become an official."

Finally, the Minister asked about Ranqiu .

The Master answered, "Ranqiu is accomplished in many ways. He too should have no difficulty."

6.9 When Minister Ji wanted to make Min Ziqian[3] the head of his Fei Estate, Min Ziqian begged the messenger to decline the

1 The bull is a metaphor for Ranyong whose origin was poor and lowly.

2 A minister of Lu.

3 Confucius' disciple.

必在汶上矣。”

6.10

伯牛有疾，子问之，自牖（yǒu）执其手，曰：“亡之，命矣夫！斯人也而有斯疾也！斯人也而有斯疾也！”

6.11

子曰：“贤哉回也！一箪（dān）食，一瓢饮，在陋巷，人不堪其忧，回也不改其乐，贤哉回也！”

6.12

冉求曰：“非不说（yuè）子之道，力不足也。”
子曰：“力不足者，中道而废。今女画。”

9.20

子曰：“语之而不惰者，其回也与！”

9.21

子谓颜渊曰：“惜乎！吾见其进也，未见其止也。”

9.27

子曰：“衣敝缊袍，与衣狐貉者立而不耻者，其由也与？‘不忮不求，

offer for him. He said, "Should someone come again with the same offer, he would find me on the northern side of the Wen River[1].

6.10 Boniu[2] became seriously ill. The Master paid him a call. Holding Boniu's hand, he said, "Alas, we are going to lose you. Such is fate. How sad that a man like you should contract such a disease! What a great misfortune!"

6.11 The Master said, "Yan Hui was truly virtuous. He had only a bamboo tube of grain to eat, a ladle of water to drink and a back alley to live in. Most people would find such a hard life intolerable. But Yan Hui did not allow it to affect his cheerfulness. How virtuous he was!"

6.12 Ranqiu said, "Not that I am unhappy with your teaching. It is just that I've run out of strength." The Master answered, "Those who have run out of their strength give up half way. You draw your limit even before starting."

9.20 The Master said, "If there's anyone who can listen to me with unflagging attention, it has to be Yan Hui."

9.21 Speaking of Yan Hui, the Master said, "Alas, he is gone. I saw him always making progress, never stopping in his effort."

9.27 The Master said, "If there is anyone wearing a worn-out gown standing beside a man dressed in fur and not feeling ashamed, I suppose it must be Zilu. 'Neither envious nor covetous, how can he be anything but good.'[3]" On hearing himself praised, Zilu

1 Implying he would flee to the State of Qi.

2 Confucius' disciple.

3 A quote from the *Book of Songs*.

何用不臧？'" 子路终身诵之。子曰："是道也，何足以臧？"

11.1

子曰："先进于礼乐，野人也；后进于礼乐，君子也。如用之，则吾从先进。"

11.2

子曰："从我于陈、蔡者，皆不及门也。"

11.3

德行：颜渊、闵子骞、冉伯牛、仲弓。言语：宰我、子贡。政事：冉有、季路。文学：子游、子夏。

11.4

子曰："回也非助我者也，于吾言无所不说。"

11.5

子曰："孝哉闵子骞！人不间于其父母昆弟之言。"

11.6

南容三复白圭，孔子以其兄之子妻之。

11.7

季康子问："弟子孰为好学？" 孔子对曰："有颜回者好学，不幸短命死矣，今也则亡。"

then frequently chanted those lines, whereupon the Master said, "Is that quality alone enough?"

11.1 The Master said, "Those who first studied the rituals and music with me were usually rustics. Those who later studied them with me were usually from the aristocracy. If I could choose between them, I would prefer the former."

11.2 The Master said, "None of those who were with me in Chen and Cai are here with me now."[1]

11.3 (The disciples each had their own outstanding points.) Virtuous in conduct, there were Yan Hui, Min Ziqian, Ran Boniu and Zhong Gong. Eloquent in speech, there were Cai Wu and Zigong. Capable in governance, there were Ranyou and Zilu. Knowledgeable in culture, there were Ziyou and Zixia.

11.4 The Master said, "Yan Hui is of no help to me. He is pleased with everything I say."

11.5 The Master said, "Min Ziqian is filial indeed. No one disagrees with his parents and brothers when they praised him."

11.6 Nan Rong read the verse about the white jade scepter over and over. Confucius therefore married his niece to him.[2]

11.7 Ji Kangzi[3] asked Confucius which of his disciples were eager to learn. The Master answered, "There was Yan Hui who was eager to learn. Unfortunately he died young. Now there is none."

---

1 Yan Hui, Zilu and Zigong had accompanied Confucius when he visited the State of Chen and Cai where they suffered hunger and other hardships. Now, Yan Hui Zilu had died and Zigong had left Confucius. The Master was thus expressing his sorrow at the loss of the two.

2 The verse in the *Book of Songs* says: One can erase a black spot on a white jade scepter, but not the flaws in one's speech.

3 Minister of Lu.

11.9

颜渊死，子曰："噫！天丧予！天丧予！"

11.10

颜渊死，子哭之恸。从者曰："子恸矣。"曰："有恸乎？非夫人之为恸而谁为？"

11.13

闵子侍侧，訚訚（yín）如也；子路，行行（hàng）如也；冉有、子贡，侃侃如也。子乐："若由也，不得其死然。"

11.14

鲁人为长府。闵子骞曰："仍旧贯，如之何？何必改作？"

子曰："夫人不言，言必有中。"

11.15

子曰："由之瑟，奚为于丘之门？"门人不敬子路。子曰："由也升堂矣，未入于室也。"

11.16

子贡问："师与商也孰贤？"

子曰："师也过，商也不及。"

曰："然则师愈与？"

11.9 When Yan Hui died, the Master said, "Alas! Heaven has destroyed me. Heaven has destroyed me."

11.10 When Yan Hui died, the Master wept bitterly. His disciples said, "Master, you are over-grieved." The Master said, "Am I? If I do not grieve for him, who else should I grieve for?"

11.13 Standing in attendance on the Master, Min Ziqian looked respectful and honest, Zilu looked firm and staunch, Ranyou and Zigong gentle and affable. The Master was pleased, but he commented, "A man like Zilu will probably not die a natural death[1]."

11.14 The Chief Minister of Lu wanted to rebuild the treasury. Min Ziqian said, "Can it not be renovated? Why must it be rebuilt?" The Master said, "Here is a man of few words. Yet when he speaks, he hits the nail on the head."

11.15 The Master said, "What is Zilu doing, playing the Se[2] in my house?" From then on, the other disciples ceased to treat Zilu with respect. The Master then said, "Zilu may have entered the main hall, but not the inner chamber."[3]

11.16 Zigong asked, "Who is the better of the two, Zizhang or Zixia?" The Master said, "Zizhang tends to go too far. With Zixia, it is not far enough."

"Does that make Zizhang better?"

---

1 Meaning he is too quick to enter a fight.

2 An ancient Chinese musical instrument similar to the zither.

3 This means Zilu has made progress but he is not yet proficient. The Master's talks were often accompanied by background music. Commentators speculated that the tune Zilu played was too militant and noisy to Confucius'taste.The Master was therefore angry at him. When he found that his disciples began to look down on Zilu, he gave the latter his due so as not to embarass him.

子曰:“过犹不及。”

11.17

季氏富于周公,而求也为之聚敛而附益之。子曰:“非吾徒也。小子鸣鼓而攻之,可也。”

11.18

柴也愚,参也鲁,师也辟,由也喭(yàn)。

11.19

子曰:“回也其庶乎,屡空。赐不受命,而货殖焉,亿则屡中。”

11.24

季子然问:“仲由、冉求可谓大臣与?”

子曰:“吾以子为异之问,曾由与求之间。所谓大臣者,以道事君,不可则止。今由与求也,可谓具臣矣。”

曰:“然则从之者与?”

子曰:“弑父与君,亦不从也。”

11.25

子路使子羔为费宰。子曰:“贼夫人之子。”

子路曰:“有民人焉,有社稷焉,何必读书,然后为学?”

子曰:“是故恶夫佞者。”

"Going too far is just as bad as not going far enough."

11.17 The Jisun Family was wealthier than the Duke of Zhou (who served in a similar post in the court of Zhou as Jisun in the court of Lu), yet Ranqiu helped them become even richer by increasing the levies. The Master said, "Ranqiu is no student of mine. Disciples, you may beat the drums and attack him."

11.18 (The Master said), "Gao Chai is dumb; Zeng Cen is slow; Zizhang goes to extremes and Zilu is rash."

11.19 The Master said, "Yan Hui's scholarship and character are near perfection, yet he is often impoverished. Zigong, not content with his lot, is engaged in trade and hoarding, yet he is often right in his speculations."

11.24 Ji Ziran[1] asked, "Could Zilu and Ranqiu be great ministers?"

The Master said, "I thought you would ask about someone else, never expecting you would mention Zilu and Ranqiu. A great minister should serve the sovereign according to the Way. If he cannot do that, he should give up his post. All one can say is that Zilu and Ranqiu are capable ministers."

Ji Ziran then asked, "In that case, would they always do what they are told to do?" The Master said, "No, not to the extent of killing their father or sovereign."

11.25 Zilu recommended Zigao to be the county magistrate of Bi. The Master said, "You are ruining someone else's son."

Zilu said, "In Bi, there are people, land and crops. Why must one study before he can be considered educated?"

The Master answered, "It is for such remarks that I dislike people

---

1 A member of the Jisun family.

11.26

子路、曾皙、冉有、公西华侍坐。子曰:“以吾一日长乎尔,毋吾以也。居则曰:‘不吾知也!’如或知尔,则何以哉?”子路率尔而对曰:“千乘之国,摄乎大国之间,加之以师旅,因之以饥馑,由也为之,比及三年,可使有勇,且知方也。”夫子哂之。

“求,尔何如?”

对曰:“方六七十,如五六十,求也为之,比及三年,可使足民。如其礼乐,以俟君子。”

“赤,尔何如?”

对曰:“非曰能之,愿学焉。宗庙之事,如会同,端章甫,愿为小相焉。”

“点,尔何如?”

鼓瑟希,铿尔,舍瑟而作,对曰:“异乎三子者之撰。”

who resort to sophistry."[1]

11.26 Zilu, Zeng Xi, Ranyou and Gongxi Hua sat in attendance on Confucius. The Master said, "Because I am slightly older than you, you should not hesitate to express yourselves. You often say, 'No one recognizes my worth!' If someone did recognize your worth, how would you serve him?"

Zilu answered without thinking, "Let's say a state of a thousand chariots is hemmed in by several large states. It is harassed by troops from outside and suffer from famine at home. If I were sent there to govern, by the end of three years, I would have been able to imbue all the people with courage and set them on the right course."

The Master smiled. He then asked, "What about you, Ranyou?"

Ranyou replied, "Let's take a small state of sixty or seventy, or even fifty or sixty square *li*. If I were to govern it, by the end of three years, I would have made everyone prosperous. As for reviving the rituals and music, that would have to wait for a wise and honorable man to come along."

The Master asked further, "And you, Gongxi Hua, what would you do?"

"Not that I'm already capable, but I would be willing to learn. At times of ancestral worship and negotiations with foreign allies, I would dress up in ceremonial robe and cap, and serve as a minor protocol official."

"And what about you, Zeng Xi?" the Master asked.

Zeng Xi was coming to the end of a piece he was playing on the *Se*. He plucked the final note and laid the instrument down.

1 Confucius disapproved of Zilu taking Zigao away from study, because Zigao was quite young then.

子曰:“何伤乎?亦各言其志也。”

曰:“莫春者,春服既成,冠者(shěn)五六人,童子六七人,浴乎沂,风乎舞雩(yú),咏而归。”

夫子喟然叹曰:“吾与点也!”

三子者出,曾皙后。曾皙曰:“夫三子者之言何如?”

子曰:“亦各言其志也已矣。”

曰:“夫子何哂由也?”

曰:“为国以礼。其言不让,是故哂之。”

“唯求则非邦也与?”

“安见方六七十如五六十而非邦也者?”

“唯赤则非邦也与?”

“宗庙会同,非诸侯而何?赤也为之小,孰能为之大?”

Rising from his seat, he replied, "My idea is very different from theirs."

The Master said, "No harm in that. After all, each of you are entitled to talk about your own aspirations."

Zeng Xi went on, "In late Spring, and everyone has put on spring clothes, I would, in the company of five or six adults and six or seven children, bathe in the Yi River and enjoy the breeze on the Rain Altar and sing our way home."

Heaving a deep sigh, the Master said, "I'm all for Zeng Xi!"

Zilu, Ranyou and Gongxi Hua then took their leave. Zeng Xi was the last to go. He asked the Master, "What do you think of my three fellow disciples' answers?"

The Master said, "Each spoke of his own aspiration, that's all."

"Why did you smile at Zilu?" Zeng Xi asked.

The Master said, "When governing a state, one must show deference for others. He was not at all modest, so I smiled at him."

"Was Ranyou really talking about governing a state?"

"Why can't a territory of sixty to seventy, or fifty to sixty square *li* be called a state?"

"Then perhaps Gongxi Hua was not talking about the same matter?" Zeng Xi asked.

The Master said, "He referred to ancestral temples and meetings with allied states. What was he talking about then if not about governing a state? If he were to act only as a minor protocol official, who would take the role of a major official?"

12.12

子曰:“片言可以折狱者,其由也与?”子路无宿诺。

13.4

樊迟请学稼。子曰:“吾不如老农。”请学为圃。曰:“吾不如老圃。”樊迟出。子曰:“小人哉,樊须也!上好礼,则民莫敢不敬,上好义,则民莫敢不服;上好信,则民莫敢不用情。夫如是,则四方之民襁负其子而至矣,焉用稼?”

14.29

子贡方人。子曰:“赐也贤乎哉?夫我则不暇。”

12.12 The Master said, "If there's anyone who can settle a litigation case on the basis of evidence provided by one party, Zilu is probably the one."

Zilu never puts off fulfilling his promises.[1]

13.4 Fan Chi asked the Master to teach him farming. The Master said, "I am not as good as an old farmer." When asked to be taught how to grow vegetables, he said, "I am not as good as a gardener." After Fan Chi had left, the Master said, "Fan Chi is indeed a petty man! If those at the top observe the rituals, the common people will not dare show irreverence. If they are upright, the common people will not dare disobey. If they promote honesty, the common people will not dare to be deceitful. If they are able to do all this, the common people everywhere will flock to them with their babies strapped on their backs. What need is there for those at the top to learn farming?"

14.29 Zigong was talking about the faults of others. The Master said, "Zigong, are you so perfect yourself? I have no time for such prattle."

---

1 Commentators find it hard to explain the logical connection between the two sentences. One explanation suggests that Zilu was quick-tempered and passed out judgement without hearng evidence by both parties to the litigation.

十四

杂集——不能归入前述章节的条目

XIV

Miscellaneous topics which do not belong to any of above categories

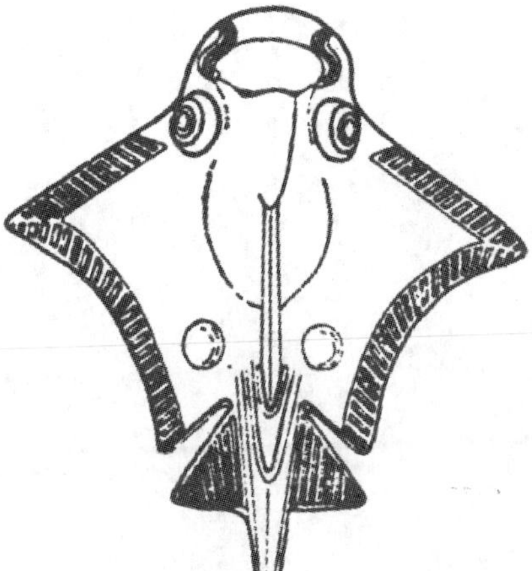

14.10

子曰:“贫而无怨难，富而无骄易。”

16.11

子曰:“见善如不及，见不善如探汤。吾见其人矣，吾闻其语矣。隐居以求其志，行义以达其道。吾闻其语矣，未见其人也。”

17.3

子曰:“唯上知与下愚不移。”

17.26

子曰:“年四十而见恶焉，其终也已。”

14.10 The Master said, "To be poor and yet not resentful is difficult. To be rich and yet not arrogant is easy."

16.11 Confucius said, "In pursuing goodness, one fears lagging behind. In avoiding vices, one stays away from them like one does boiling water. I have heard this said and seen it practised. To live in seclusion in order to strengthen one's aspiration; to follow what is righteous in order to realize the Way. I have heard this said, but I have never seen such a person."

17.3 The Master said, "Only the intelligent elite and the ignorant masses will never change."

17.26 The Master said, "He who is still disliked at the age of forty has no hope left."

Chronicle
Major Events in the Life of Confucius

551**BC** Confucius (Chinese name Kong Qiu 孔丘) was born in the town of Zou, in the State of Lu.

549**BC** Confucius' father Kong He (孔纥, also known as Shuliang He 叔梁纥) died when he was only three years old. His Mother, Yan Zhengzai (颜徵在), took him back to her native place, Qufu, the capital of Lu.

548-536**BC** Confucius was a studious child. Guided by his mother, Confucius distinguished himself in his studies at a very young age.

535BC His mother passed away.

533BC Confucius married. His wife was surnamed Qi (亓).

532BC Confucius began to take up minor offices in the government. His first job was being in charge of warehouses (later, animal husbandry). That year, his son Boyu was born. (Confucius also had two daughters, but their names and dates of birth were unknown.)

522BC Confucius began private tutoring around this time, his earliest disciples being Yan Hui and Zilu.

517-516BC Confucius went to the State of Qi where he was granted an interview by Duke Jing. Since the latter would not give him office, Confucius returned to Lu.

501BC Confucius was appointed head of Zhongdu County.

500BC Confucius was appointed Minister of Justice. He initiated many reforms. He also distinguished himself during an official meeting between Duke Ding of Lu and Duke Jing of Qi.

497BC Disheartened by the failure of Duke Ding and his chief ministers to carry out the reforms he proposed, Confucius left the State of Lu.

497-484BC For fourteen years Confucius and his disciples toured the states of Wei, Chen, Cai and others, propagating his political and ethical ideas. However, the rulers of these states either declined to support them or were half-hearted in their backing.

485BC Confucius' wife died while he was away from home.

483BC Confucius returned to Lu. He was no longer interested in taking up office in the government. He continued to teach and edit the classics. His son Boyu died.

481BC To his great sorrow, his favorite disciple Yan Hui died at the age of 41.

480BC His disciple Zilu, also very close to him, was killed in a palace intrigue in the state of Wei.

479BC Saddened by these developments which impaired his health, Confucius died at the age of 73. Many of his disciples stayed at his graveside for three years, following the rituals of the times. They later moved to various states to propagate his teachings, spreading his influence throughout ancient China.

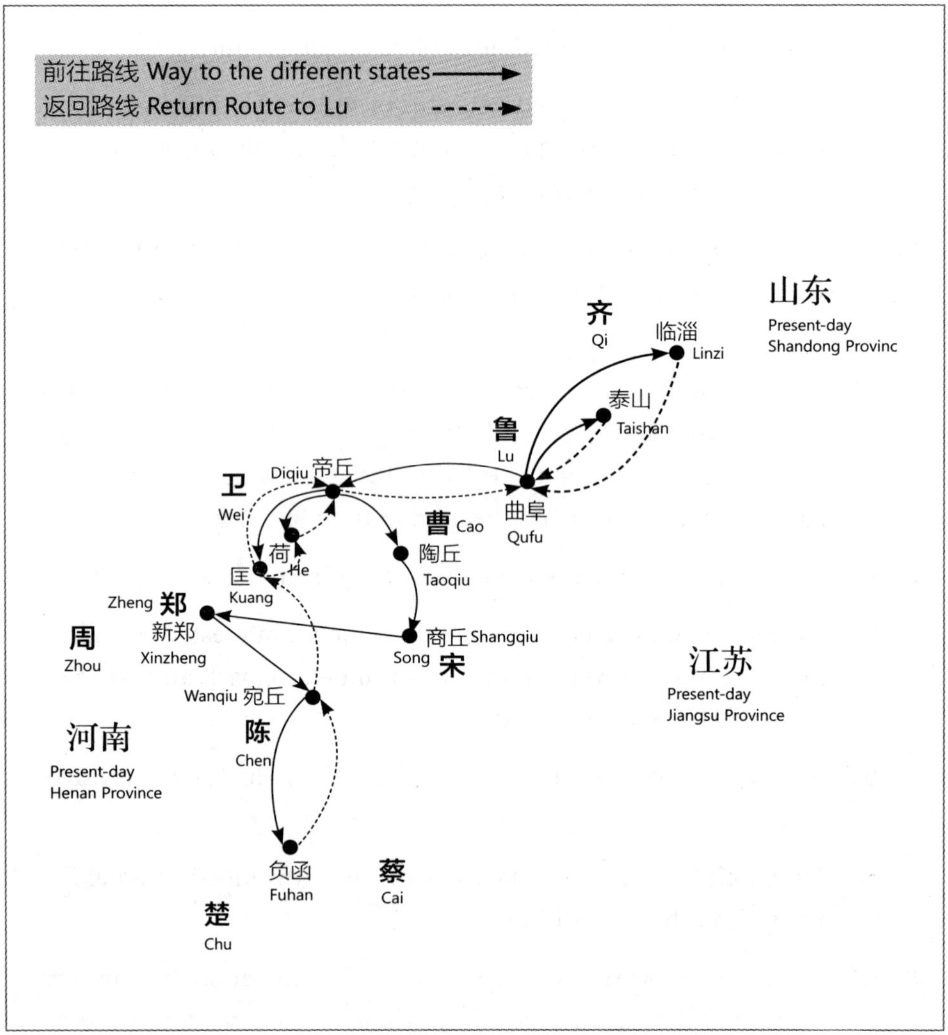

前往路线 Way to the different states
返回路线 Return Route to Lu
齐
Qi
临淄
Linzi
山东
Present-day
Shandong Provinc
泰山
Taishan
鲁
Lu
曲阜
Qufu
卫
Wei
Diqiu 帝丘
荷
He
匡
Kuang
曹 Cao
陶丘
Taoqiu
Zheng 郑
新郑
Xinzheng
周
Zhou
商丘 Shangqiu
Song 宋
江苏
Present-day
Jiangsu Province
Wanqiu 宛丘
陈
Chen
河南
Present-day
Henan Province
负函
Fuhan
蔡
Cai
楚
Chu

Confucius Says
Thirty Useful Quotations from *The Analects*

1 The Master said, "Is it not a great pleasure to be able to practice frequently what you have learned? Is it not a real delight to have friends come to visit you from afar? Is it not the mark of a man of honor (君子 *junzi*) to not take offence when others fail to appreciate your worth?" (1.1)

子曰："学而时习之，不亦悦乎？有朋自远方来，不亦乐乎？人不知而不愠，不亦君子乎？"（1.1）

2 The Master said, "Do not worry about not being appreciated by others. Rather, worry about your not being able to appreciate them." (1.16)

子曰："不患人之不己知，患不知人也。"（1.16）

3 The Master said, "When I reached 15, I began devoting myself to learning. At 30, I could stand on my own. At 40, my mind was no longer confused. At 50, I knew what Heaven demanded of me. At 60, I was able to distinguish right from wrong in what other people told me. And since 70, I have been able to follow my heart's desire without transgressing the rules."(2.4)

子曰："吾十有五而志于学，三十而立，四十而不惑，五十而知天命，六十而耳顺，七十而从心所欲，不逾矩。"（2.4）

4 The Master said, "Observe a person's behavior, find out what leads him to behave the way he does and see what he rests content with. If one does that, how can that person still manage to hide his true character? How indeed?" (2.10)

子曰："视其所以，观其所由，察其所安，人焉叟哉？人焉叟哉？"(2.10)

5 The Master said, "A man of honor associates with many but does not form a clique; the petty-minded man (小人 *xiaoren*) does the opposite." (2.14)

子曰："君子周而不比，小人比而不周。"(2.14)

6 The Master said, "Learning without reflection will end up in confusion; reflection without learning will end up in peril." (2.15)

子曰："学而不思则罔，思而不学则殆。"(2.15)

7 The Master said, "Zilu, shall I tell you what true knowledge is? Say you know when you know, and say you don't know when you don't, that is true knowledge." (2.17)

子曰："由！诲女知之乎？知之为知之，不知为不知，是知也。"(2.17)

8 The Master said, "How can a person get on if he is not trustworthy? It is just like a cart without a collar-bar or a carriage without a yoke-bar. How can he make it move?" (2.22)

子曰："人而无信，不知其可也。大车无輗，小车无軏，其何以行之哉？"(2.22)

9 The Master said, "Do not worry about not having an official position. Worry about whether you are qualified for such a position. Do not worry when others don't appreciate your work. Rather, try to be worthy of being appreciated." (4.14)

子曰："不患无位，患所以立。不患莫己知，求为可知也。"（4.14）

10 The Master said, "When you meet a man of virtue, think how you can become his equal; when you meet a man without virtue, examine yourself to see if you are the same. (4.17)

子曰："见贤思齐焉，见不贤而内自省也。"（4.17）

11 The Master said, "I do not try to enlighten my disciples until they have tried hard but failed to understand something. I do not supply my disciples with any new vocabulary or put their ideas into words for them unless they have difficulty doing so. When I have given them one instance and they cannot draw inferences from it, I do not repeat my lesson." (7.8)

子曰："不愤不启，不悱不发。举一隅不以三隅反，则不复也。"（7.8）

12 The Master said, "Walking in the company of others, there is bound to be something I can learn from them. Their good traits I follow; their bad ones I try to avoid." (7.22)

子曰："三人行，必有我师焉：择其善者而从之，其不善者而改之。"（7.22）

13 The Master said, "It's like building a mound. If I stopped before the last basket of earth, I would never complete the job. It's like

filling a hollow. Even if I have tipped in only the first basketful of earth, it would be a step forward if I kept at it." (9.19)

子曰："譬如为山，未成一篑，止，吾止也。譬如平地，虽覆一篑，进，吾往也。"（9.19）

14 The Master said, "The young should be regarded with awe. How do we know the next generation will not surpass the present? Those who have reached the age of forty or fifty, yet still haven't achieved anything to distinguish themselves, need not be taken seriously." (9.23)

子曰："后生可畏，焉知来者之不如今也？四十、五十而无闻焉，斯亦不足畏也已。"（9.23）

15 The Master said, "You can deprive an army of its commanding officer, but you cannot deprive a man of his aspirations." (9.26)

子曰："三军可夺帅也，匹夫不可夺志也。"（9.26）

16 The Master said, "Only in the cold of winter is the point brought home that pines and cypresses are the last to fade." (9.28)

子曰："岁寒，然后知松柏之后彫也。"（9.28）

17 The Master said, "Going too far is just as bad as not going far enough." (11.16)

子曰："过犹不及。"（11.16）

18 The Master said, "A man of honor helps others to realize their best aims, but not their worst desires. A petty-minded man does

the opposite." (12.16)

子曰："君子成人之美，不成人之恶。小人反是。"（12.16）

19 The Master said, "If a ruler is correct in his own behavior, then people will obey him without him giving any orders, but if he misbehaves, people will not obey him even if he issued orders." (13.6)

子曰："其身正，不令而行；其身不正，虽令不从。"（13.6）

20 The Master said, "To fail to advise a person who can benefit from it is to let that person go to waste. To advise a person who cannot benefit from it is to let your words go to waste. A wise man will waste neither man nor words." (15.8)

子曰："可与言而不与之言，失人；不可与言而与之言，失言。知者不失人，亦不失言。"（15.8）

21 The Master said, "Use the calendar of Xia, ride in the carriage of Yin, and wear the ceremonial cap of Zhou. As for music, play the *Shao* and *Wu*, abandon the tunes of *Zheng* and stay away from the flatterers. The tunes of *Zheng* are lascivious and the flatterers are dangerous." (15.11)

子曰："行夏之时，乘殷之辂，服周之冕，乐则《韶》、《舞》。放郑声，远佞人。郑声淫，佞人殆。"（15.11）

22 The Master said, "Sorrow awaits those who don't take a long view." (15.12)

子曰："人无远虑，必有近忧。"（15.12）

23 The Master said, "A man of honor fears his own insufficiencies, not the failure of others to understand him." (15.19)

子曰："君子病无能焉，不病人之不己知也。"（15.19）

24 The Master said, "A man of honor does not approve of a person because he expresses an opinion to his liking, nor does he reject an opinion because it is held by a person he dislikes." (15.23)

子曰："君子不以言举人，不以人废言。"（15.23）

25 The Master said, "Be sure to look into a person's case when everyone dislikes him. The same when everyone seems to like him." (15.28)

子曰："众恶之，必察焉；众好之，必察焉。"（15.28）

26 The Master said, "A mistake not corrected is a mistake indeed." (15.30)

子曰："过而不改，是谓过矣。"（15.30）

27 The Master said, "Where humaneness is concerned, be not afraid to overtake your master." (15.36)

子曰："当仁不让于师。"（15.36）

28 The Master said, "In teaching, I take disciples of all background without discrimination." (15.39)

子曰："有教无类。"（15.39）

29 Confucius said, "It is beneficial to make friends with three types of people: the upright, the trustworthy and the well-informed. It

is harmful to make friends with three other types: the obsequious, the double-faced and the smooth-tongued." (16.4)

孔子曰："益者三友，损者三友。友直，友谅，友多闻，益矣。友便辟，友善柔，友便佞，损矣。"（16.4）

30 Confucius said, "There are beneficial and harmful pleasures. To be restrained by music and rituals, to praise other people's virtues and to befriend worthy people—these are beneficial pleasures. To be soothed by licentious sounds, to idle away time and to indulge in banqueting—these are harmful pleasures." (16.5)

孔子曰："益者三乐，损者三乐。乐节礼乐，乐道人之善，乐多贤友，益矣。乐骄乐，乐佚游，乐宴乐，损矣。"（16.5）

Index

I. Historical figures

II. Confucius' disciples

III. Key Terminologies

图书在版编目（CIP）数据

论语新解全译：汉英对照／林戊荪编译．—北京：外文出版社，2016.
ISBN 978-7-119-10543-7

I. ①论… II. ①林… III. ①儒家 ②《论语》—注释—汉、英 ③《论语》—译文—汉、英 IV. ① B222.2

中国版本图书馆 CIP 数据核字（2016）第 253937 号

责任编辑 刘 波
封面设计 柏拉图设计工作室
印刷监制 冯 浩

论语新解全译

林戊荪 编译

出 版 人 徐 步
出版发行 外文出版社有限责任公司
地　　址 北京市西城区百万庄大街 24 号 **邮政编码** 100037
网　　址 http://www.flp.com.cn **电子邮箱** flp@cipg.org.cn
电　　话 008610-68320579（总编室） 008610-68996177（编辑部）
008610-68995852（发行部） 008610-68996183（投稿电话）
印　　刷 北京飞达印刷责任有限公司
经　　销 新华书店／外文书店
开　　本 700mm×1000mm 1/16
印　　张 21.5
字　　数 150 千字
版　　次 2020 年 1 月第 1 版第 2 次印刷
书　　号 ISBN 978-7-119-10543-7
定　　价 80.00 元